Impossible Objects

Impossible Objects
Interviews

———

Simon Critchley

Edited by Carl Cederström and Todd Kesselman

polity

First published in 2012 by Polity Press

Polity Press
65 Bridge Street
Cambridge CB2 1UR, UK

Polity Press
350 Main Street
Malden, MA 02148, USA

ISBN-13: 978-0-7456-5320-4
ISBN-13: 978-0-7456-5321-1 (pb)

A catalog record for this book is available from the British Library.

Typeset in 12 on 14 pt Bembo
by Servis Filmsetting Ltd, Stockport, Cheshire
Printed and bound in Great Britain by the MPG Books Group

The publisher has used its best endeavors to ensure that the URLs for external websites referred to in this book are correct and active at the time of going to press. However, the publisher has no responsibility for the websites and can make no guarantee that a site will remain live or that the content is or will remain appropriate.

Every effort has been made to trace all copyright holders, but if any have been inadvertently overlooked the publisher will be pleased to include any necessary credits in any subsequent reprint or edition.

For further information on Polity, visit our website: www.politybooks.com

Contents

Introduction

In the time that it takes the word "philosophy" to leap off the written page, onto the glassy surface of your eye, and down that astonishingly complex and dark tunnel that we call the mind, most of us have already conjured up a few definite associations: timeless, absolute, true without qualification. Philosophy is *supposed to be* about those things we need to be most certain about, those categories or concepts where the stakes are the highest, and which determine what it means to be human, to be alive, to be on this planet. For this reason, and understandably so, most philosophers are intellectually constipated: they are more than reluctant to say anything out loud unless they are sure that they want it to ring eternally in the hallowed halls of the academy. For the philosopher, to speak is a great risk; it is to risk everything, insofar as once one has spoken, one puts in jeopardy everything that one has already said, and everything that one will say. To risk error is to risk eternity. And what could be more frightening than that.

The interview, one might say then, is for the philosopher a battlefield of anxiety, where one forgoes the right to retreat into one's quiet study of peaceful contemplation, where one is forced to speak before one knows the real consequences of one's words, where one's mouth might threaten to betray one's mind, or even one's system of thought. It is the place where opinion muddles the clarity of 'pure' thinking – whatever that might be – and where one is forced to take a stance on the world in one's own time. There should be nothing more terrifying to the philosopher, and indeed, nothing more important.

It is in this spirit that the interviews presented here have been gathered and collated. They aim to trace the risk of thinking out loud and with others, within the process of developing ideas and perspectives, for better or worse, until death do us part. This process exemplifies the meaning of what philosophy, for some of us, might be about: our stake in the world, our exchange with others, the movement and praxis of thinking itself.

We originally intended this collection as an appendix to the work of Simon Critchley, but it could also be read in another way. What the written word often tries to conceal is that philosophy does not descend upon us from up on high but, rather, develops, undergoes modifications, and takes its time in doing so. This activity, this struggle in thought, in its time, constitutes the very essence of the activity that is philosophy. As surprising as this may be, its resistance to setting down a final, permanent encampment is intrinsic to it, even if this has been something that has been historically resisted, rejected, denied, and suppressed. The idea that philosophy should only appear in print, when all accounts have been settled and when all debates have been resolved, is itself nothing more than the perverse fantasy of a certain erroneous vision of philosophy that holds onto certainty like a petulant child. In this light, the interview can hardly be a *mere* appendix.

If the tired old cliché of philosophical withholding could be called anal-ytic, the interviews collected here are unapologetically – to use a Heideggerian trope – diarrhetic. They are playful, at times provocative, at times entertaining, but in each case oriented towards the task of genuine thinking, by which we mean thinking that does not simply rest upon what has been said before, but aims to open up new territories, and agitate outdated philosophical platitudes. In this sense, these interviews represent thinking as a form of labor; an intellectual *work*, or working-through. This is, we submit, another possibility to consider, the next time the word philosophy should pass through the digestive tract of your psyche.

As Simon Critchley has been interviewed frequently over the last two decades, we were faced with an over-brimming collection of material in bringing this volume to fruition. The selections we have made were based primarily on two criteria; that they cover a reasonably diverse span within Critchley's work, both topically and temporally. The present volume consists in nine interviews, six of which have been published elsewhere in various mediums, and three of which appear here for the first time. With regard to those interviews that have appeared elsewhere, we have taken the liberty of occasionally removing certain passages solely for the purpose of avoiding repetition amongst the different interviews. We have tried, as much as possible, to preserve the original character and flow of each interview in order to maintain the spirit in which it took place.

With the intention of providing some context for the material, each of the interviews is preceded by a short introduction, interspersed with Critchley's own comments and reflections. More than ten years separate the first interview from the last, and, in this respect, the reader will find a shift in philosophical interests: the most recent interview on tragedy concerns material that is still being thought through, while the earliest (from 2000) deals with questions that are no longer as central to his current perspective.

We should also say something about the title, *Impossible Objects*. The term comes from an abandoned project, at the bottom of one of those drawers that most of us have, and in this case it happens to have been from Simon's. The book was to have been called *Paraphilosophy*, and it was to have been a catalogue of those themes that stubbornly resist definition and simple appropriation. At the time, three paradigmatic domains presented themselves: poetry, humor, and music. Along with these, the themes presented in this collection – art, deconstruction, political resistance, and tragedy, just to name a few – seem to partake of this same stubborn quality, and for this reason they seem to be appropriate amendments in the field of impossibility. To quote from Simon's deserted introduction: "These paraphilosophical fragments were meant to be a collection of tiny ladders that should be kicked away in order to look directly at those things of which it is not possible to speak. The point is to let things speak for themselves. Sadly, this is easier said than done." Since the objects tend to remain quiet, it is fortunate that Critchley has not.

Finally, we would like to thank Liam Gillick for his visual genius in general, and, more specifically, for designing the cover of the book, along with Emma Hutchinson at Polity for her help in culling the vast amounts of textual material, and, moreover, for her infinite patience with us. We would also like to thank each interviewer for making this project possible, and for allowing us to include their work in this volume. And last but not least, a thank you to Simon for his openness in this collaboration, and for giving us so many words to choose from.

Carl Cederström and Todd Kesselman

1 Early Bedfellows

Levinas, Derrida, and the Ethics of Deconstruction

Joshua Mullan and David Hannigan

Sydney, Australia, April 2000

This is one of the earliest recorded interviews with Simon Critchley. David Hannigan and Joshua Mullan were two PhD students at the University of Sydney whom Critchley had met on a couple of occasions, and were "serious about having a philosophical conversation." The interview took place in April of 2000, while Critchley was a visiting scholar in the philosophy department at the University of Sydney. The setting was idyllic.

> *It took place in the office of Moira Gatens, which I was borrowing for the semester, in the Old Building, which is this beautiful mid-nineteenth century imitation of an Oxford college, on a hill just to the north of Sydney, but on the edge of the city. There was this Jacaranda tree in the quad outside, and these birds would screech and hop around out there.*

The discussion focuses on Critchley's first published book, The Ethics of Deconstruction, *which had been based upon his PhD thesis. The great achievement of that book was that it had, for the first time, opened up an ethical reading of Derrida and deconstruction through the work of Levinas. This ethical reading was a significant contribution in that Derrida was routinely dismissed as an empty formalist, or perhaps even a nihilist. In this interview, we find a detailed account of the shaping of these early thoughts. "It is a very accurate overview of what I was thinking in the context of*

5

the Ethics of Deconstruction.*" But it also extends the original arguments, relating them to key themes of the Frankfurt School, especially the work of Jürgen Habermas. A few years prior to the interview, in 1997, Critchley had spent a full year in Frankfurt, debating and working with Axel Honneth. "You can see the extent of the influence the Frankfurt School debates had on me at the time." Honneth's inheritance of Habermas is explored here as a means to bridge the gap between ethical subjectivity and political formalism – a line of thought that also appeared in Critchley's* Continental Philosophy, *but later receded within his work. "I recall that the conversation was very intense and focused, but I couldn't even do this interview now. The material isn't present in my mind any longer. It's interesting to see how the interview is a kind of slice of time, what one was thinking about at a certain period, and the way that the themes accumulate and pile up." The interview is here published for the first time, as it had not been carried out with the intention of publication. "I am very pleased that something is finally happening with it. David and Josh spoke with me for their own curiosity, but they were extremely professional, and the result is a good portrait of some of my early obsessions."*

DAVID HANNIGAN: Given that much of your work to date has revolved around the writings of Emmanuel Levinas and Jacques Derrida, can you please tell us when, and in what circumstances, you first encountered their work?

SIMON CRITCHLEY: I purchased a copy of *Totality and Infinity* at a book sale in 1983, which cost almost nothing. I remember reading the preface on the train from Colchester to London and thinking, "This is amazing." I knew Buber's work at the time and had been very persuaded by *I and Thou* and so I fitted Levinas into the context of Buber and the Jewish tradition straight away. Derrida, I can remember to this day, I read in a launderette in the University of Essex. Again that was in 1983. We were reading "Structure, Sign, and Play in the Human Sciences" in the Communist Society reading group at Essex University, which seems faintly comical now. We were very serious. I read that essay and hadn't really understood it. Then I read the opening page of "Violence and Metaphysics" on Levinas and thought that the first paragraph, where Derrida is talking about the question, the community of the question and all that, was simply extraordinary. Derrida was the avant-garde in continental philosophy and therefore I wanted to understand it. Also, the assumption we shared, without knowing much, was that Derrida was somebody on the left; we read his work in the Communist Society reading group after reading Althusser and Foucault and therefore his works would have had obvious ethical and political relevance. So that's how I came to them.

JOSHUA MULLAN: And it was out of that context that your initial thesis emerged?

SC: Yes. The problem for me in Derrida's work was, what prevents this form of reading from simply being a textual formalism without any relevance to contextual questions of ethics, culture, society, politics? I tried to show that the basic operation in his thought is ethical. That deconstruction as a practice of reading is ethical, which was also a claim being advanced by Hillis Miller at about the same time. But I was always a long, long way from the preoccupations of the Yale School. I wanted to make the more substantive claim that there was a phenomenology of moral experience – well, almost – in Derrida's work, provided you read it in relationship to Levinas. So the idea was that we can save Derrida's work from what looked like an empty formalism, which was the Hegelian critique of Derrida by people like Jay Bernstein and Gillian Rose at that time in the UK. And we can do this by showing that there was an ethical motivation to his work, with possible political consequences. So that was the specific

7

agenda for writing *The Ethics of Deconstruction* and that was there from very early on. And it is interesting how differently Derrida's work appears now than it did in the 1980s.

DH: More recently, you have stated that you are more doubtful about the persuasive force of Levinasian ethics. Why?

SC: In many ways the context changed. In the late 1980s, if you were interested in Levinas, you felt that you were part of a tiny clique who read these texts with an almost religious fervor. It seemed as if there were maybe ten people in the world who really took Levinas seriously. The way in which Levinas came into focus for many people was through the success of Derrida's work. And people like me and my supervisor Robert Bernasconi and others were trying to present Levinas's thought and defend it to the hilt against ignorance of his work. I think the key experience here was the Heidegger affair in 1986–7 and the Paul de Man affair in 1987. The claim was that deconstruction in its Heideggerian or De Manian forms was morally vacuous. In that context, and for people who were accused of that, Levinas became a very useful way of showing that there was a post-Heideggerian ethics or a deconstructive ethics. So that was the context, and what changed for me was that the consensus changed. Levinas became available, even trendy, as a philosopher and the critical, philosophical task became one of trying to think through what could and could not be philosophically defended in Levinas's work.

JM: What do you think about the increased interest in Levinasian ethics?

SC: It both delights and worries me. I am pleased that people are reading Levinas and not merely in philosophy but in law and in international relations, literary theory, aesthetic theory, all over the place. But there is a sense in which there is a piety that has grown up around Levinas. People are using Levinas as an intellectual crutch to stop them from doing a lot more difficult thinking. That worries me; I'm enough of a Habermasian, finally enough of a Kantian, to realize that ethics and normativity require a lot more rational discursive work than just appealing to some notion of experience of the other as immediately given. Even more worrying for me is that the category of ethics in Levinas is dependent on the category of the religious. And the way in which Levinas is picked up, particularly in the United States, as an ethical thinker is also fundamentally as a religious thinker, even in people as sophisticated as John Caputo. I think in a sense they are right that the face-to-face relation opens onto the relation of the divine in Levinas. However, as an atheist I find that unintelligible. So I want to defend Levinas in terms that show that his thought is not reliant on some type of implicit religiosity.

JM: Taking account of how your views have been modified in relation to Levinasian ethics, what do you consider to be the most significant difference between the work of Derrida and Levinas today?

SC: Well, Derrida famously says, in a 1986 discussion in Paris, that there are no differences between himself and Levinas. So in that sense there are no differences and one way of looking at Derrida's work since 1986 is in terms of making good on that statement. Also, one fairly conventional but powerful way of looking at Derrida's work is that it moves between two poles of attraction. One pole of attraction is Heideggerian and the other pole is Levinasian. I'm thinking about Levinas's skepticism concerning the place where Heidegger's movement of thought ends up – particularly with regard to ethics and politics. So, when Derrida says something like "deconstruction is justice and justice is undeconstructible" and that what justice means really is the relation to the other, then it seems to be fairly clear where he is speaking from – and that cannot be from a Heideggerian place. Heidegger would never have said anything like that. But the way Derrida gets to that statement is often still by employing Heideggerian methods or habits of thought. Derrida will still make Heideggerian moves in the argumentation but then the conclusion of the argument has a much more Levinasian feel. On the other hand, there are significant differences between Derrida and Levinas. As I see it, there are a number of problem areas in Levinas's work, specifically the question of "monotheism," the question of "sexual difference," the question of the "family" and the question of "Israel." In many ways the name "Israel" is the culmination of all those many questions. "Israel" is the name for a monotheistic political community based upon a certain conception of the family, and a very traditional understanding of sexual difference. In the face of those worries about Levinas, Derrida can be thought of as being simply critical of Levinas. However, the way he makes that critique in *Adieu: Emmanuel Levinas*, the 1997 text, is that he will say that the form of the ethical relation is right but the political content in Levinas's work is misguided. Of course, he doesn't say it as brutally as that but that's clearly what is on his mind. For me that is the significant difference between them.

DH: How do you account for what you've referred to as Levinas's political blind spot in relation to Israel? How does this relate to his views on Marxism?

SC: For Levinas, Marxism is the absorption of the ethical into the socioeconomic, and so it is the disappearance of the face-to-face relation and the privileging of relations of solidarity and anonymous sociality – what he calls, in *Time and the Other,* "socialism." And he would want to criticize Marxism from that point of view. In Levinas's own theory the name of the blind spot is "Israel." Levinas is absolutely clear from very early on that the form of the ethical relation has to be concretized and contextualized in politics, in a workable conception of justice. This is the core of his disagreement with Buber. And the name for the community that would instantiate justice informed by the ethical relation has to be "Israel" for Levinas. "Israel" means the ethically informed community of the people of the Bible. The basic message of the Bible for Levinas is the ethical relation; infinite responsibility, which leads to a certain conception of justice. And that's a conception of justice that was binding on Israel, Jewish and non-Jewish. So far, so good. "Israel" is the name for an idea of justice, a utopian idea of justice, which it was before 1948. Israel as an *actually existing state* leads Levinas into all sorts of problems, I think. He cannot criticize Israel because Israel has to be the ethical instantiation of justice in the world. Therefore when Israel commits acts of political murder, even by proxy (as it did in Sabra and Chatila in 1982, and as it has done against the Palestinians systematically since the establishment of the state of Israel), Levinas cannot criticize Israel, he doesn't have the resources for criticizing Israel. So the blind spot is structural in Levinas; it is a consequence of his movement of thought. Therefore to reveal that blind spot, to call it into question, is to call Levinas into question in a certain way.

DH: What is it that stops Derrida from having the same blind spot? Is it his ability to hesitate about political content?

SC: Not just that. To go back to what I was saying before, the accusation of formalism against Derrida, which people like me try to defend him against, is, in a sense, true. He is a formalist. There is an ethical formalism in Derrida and what is formal is a priori, it is universal, it is not context specific, so that Derrida can say that deconstruction is justice and, at all times and all places in the earth, there is this injustice which requires us to think of what justice means and to instantiate justice in the world. So there is a context-transcendent basis, in Habermasian terms, for political and social thought in Derrida. For Derrida, the question of politics becomes a question of a form of political action that would not be instantiated in some sort of organic notion of community or some existing notion of the state. The way that I have tried to think about this is to think of Derrida's notion of "democracy to come" as an ethical criterion for politicization, a movement of politicization that would be consistently challenging any notion of the state apparatus, or any notion of the community. So deconstruction in that sense becomes a form of ethical aggravation within a social context. And it is inconceivable for me that Derrida would end up endorsing any particular name like "Israel" or the way that Heidegger endorses Hölderlin's word *Germanien*. This leads Derrida into what he calls the "New International": a new form of alliance that would not be a form of alliance, or would not be specific to any particular community. So his formalism leads to a form of "political internationalism."

JM: On this point, you argued in the first edition of *The Ethics of Deconstruction* that there was an impasse of the political in Derrida's work, and that deconstruction fails to offer a coherent account of the passage from ethical responsibility to the question of the political and critique. In the second edition, you state that, based upon Derrida's work since 1992, you are more positive about the political possibilities of deconstruction. Do you remain as optimistic today?

SC: Yes I do. As other people seem to like Derrida less and become increasingly bored with him, I like him more and more. I think Derrida is simply the most intelligent philosopher that I have ever read or heard; his capacity to develop thinking, improvise thinking, assimilate concepts, and generate new ideas is absolutely extraordinary. I think he is exemplary as a philosopher. He's a bit like Miles Davis in the 1960s. On the basis of a very simple theme, he manages to elaborate an enormously complex and interesting structure and no one else can do that. No one else for me comes close to him in terms of his intellectual brilliance. The problem is that he writes too much. The worry that I had in my first book was that there was no way of getting from ethics to politics in his work. He was content to raise the question of the "question of the question" as it were, the question of responsibility prior to questioning, but failed to ask the question of politics, of what justice is, i.e., what should be done in this particular context in this particular time? He appeared to be shy of concrete political questions. But that was before the "Force of Law," *Specters of Marx, Politics of Friendship*, and a whole range of other texts. I think that in those texts he has gone an enormous way to answering some of those worries that I had.

DH: In terms of the ethical relationship to the other, the experience of the undecidable, and the legal and political decisions that are still required to be taken, could you clarify what you mean by the expression "the other's decision in me"?

SC: The "other's decision in me" is a phrase lifted from *The Politics of Friendship*. The question is very simple, namely that the traditional conception of the political in Carl Schmitt is the capacity to decide, and the fundamental decision is the decision of who is my friend and who is my enemy. Derrida's claim in *The Politics of Friendship* is that this notion of the political presupposes a conception of the subject as an active, willful, masculine actor. So the traditional conception of the political presupposes a masculine social actor who can decide who is my friend, who is my enemy. What Derrida is trying to do is criticize that notion of the political through an ethical criterion. So the activity of politics becomes conditioned by a fundamental passivity that is unconditional, which as it were is there before me and despite me. Fundamentally, there is a powerlessness, an impotence, a lack of virility that defines the subject. The subject is defined, not by the capacity to decide, but by the other's decision, which was already in me, in a way that traumatizes me. I want to link that notion in Derrida to the theme of the traumatized subject in Levinas and in psychoanalysis. To do so is to try to come up with a different picture of the subject and then to link that notion of the "other's decision in me" to a conception of political action. So political action would be invention on the basis of the "other's decision in me" – acts of invention or imagination where I create a norm, or I bring about a norm that is not necessarily foundationally deduced from a normative framework as it would be in Habermas. Here, the notion of invention or political imagination is rooted in some ethical criterion that leads me into making that decision.

JM: How might Derrida's account of the "moment of madness" in the decision be understood in relation to your understanding Badiou's Event and the psychoanalytical account of subjectivity that you offer?

SC: My interest in Badiou's work is sort of a troublemaking interest because Badiou and Derrida have not been the best of friends in the past. Insofar as one can apply the friend/enemy distinction, they are political enemies. What is fascinating in Badiou is the way in which he gives us a theory of the event, and the way in which the subject assumes the event and acts on the basis of the event. My critique of Badiou is that the

notion of politics still remains locked up in a heroic and arguably masculinist model. But I think that what Badiou can
provide is, in a sense, a way out of the impasse of Derrida's
work in terms of the theory of the event.

DH: Recalling that Badiou is so dismissive of Levinas and the
theological aspect in his work, I'm wondering about Derrida's
use of the term, the "messianic." Given the word's obvious
religious associations, do you think it is a strategically useful
notion to be used in relation to political decision-making, to
"democracy to come," to the "New International," etc.?

SC: Maybe it isn't the right word to use. I have tried to
argue in an essay on Badiou that there's a structural Judaism
at work in thinkers like Levinas and Derrida. And what I
mean by that is that the notion of the "messianic" is the idea
of the subject being constituted in relationship to an event
that overwhelms it. So the subject comes to itself, finds itself,
in relationship to an event in which it is already inscribed –
always already. Judaism is this binding oneself to a law, to
that with which you are already contracted or covenanted
in some way. The trauma has already taken place and the
subject is, as Freud says, *nachträglich*. Derrida claims that his
use of the "messianic" is in terms of a weak messianic power
in Benjamin's sense or is a "messianism without messianism."
As though there is no content, as if it is an entirely formal a
priori claim. However, I want to claim that the experience
of transcendence, which Derrida wants to evoke with the
notion of the messianic, does draw on a religious experience
– a specifically Judaic religious experience. So Badiou is right
in suspecting that there's arguably a religious motivation to
the work of Levinas and Derrida. But I think that there is
also a religious motivation to Badiou's own work. There is a
structural Christianity at work.

JM: So, is the category of the political thinkable apart from the religious?

SC: Paradoxically, I think it has to be and it is not. For me, as an old-fashioned sort of modernist, philosophy can neither continue with religion nor without religion. We require religious categories in order to think through certain issues, political issues. Yet these categories are ones that we can no longer use, so we are in an *aporia*, or simply in a mess. This means that the project of secularism is as yet unachieved, as I see it. The currently fashionable notion of the "post-secular" has no meaning. We are still decidedly pre-secular and that is the problem.

JM: And is this then why you have chosen to adopt the term "austere messianism"?

SC: I want to have my cake and eat it. I'm committed to a paradox, which is that when philosophy becomes divorced from religious categories and from religious passion, it simply becomes an exercise in technically improving common sense. Philosophy, without religion, risks becoming a technically sharpened common sense or the application of logical procedure and method to thinking. So, on the one hand, I want to say that philosophy finds the basis for passionate commitment in religious categories, but those religious categories are ones that have no content for us because we know too much. It is just too late for us.

DH: You have suggested that "The New International" can be seen as a reactivation or rearticulation of the emancipatory promise of modernity. Could you clarify what you mean by this?

SC: If there was a consensus around *Specters of Marx*, then it was that it was a good thing that Derrida was talking about

Marx and about time too: "thanks for making the effort, Jacques." However, the notion of "The New International" was treated with a lot of suspicion. It was seen as a vague posture. Now I'm less persuaded of that. I think that "The New International" is Derrida's attempt to give a political content to these formal claims about justice and ethics. And he's in a quandary, namely that political content cannot be guaranteed at the level of the state, the nation, or the community. That is probably uncontroversial. Further, there is a critique of the notion of the party. So "The New International" becomes a formal device for thinking about a collectivity – a transnational collectivity – that would not be reducible to a traditional notion of the party form. I have a problem with that. I think that the notion of party form is both more malleable than Derrida imagines, for good and ill, and it is also a necessity when we think about political action within a state, which is still, for good or ill, the current horizon for politics, even within the European Union. So I wouldn't be as skeptical about the party form as Derrida would. What I have come to think about recently in relationship to "The New International" is that there are two movements of politicization for me. There is politicization at the level of civil society, new social movements and forms of protest internal to civil society that we can think of as micro-political movements, and on the other hand the macro-political, transnational movements of identification, democratization. And what I am thinking about politically is how those two movements might come together, how transnational movements of protest or resistance might be embedded in forms of local civil protest. The basis for those two axes of politicization, it seems to me, is an ethical basis, which can be expressed in the rather nebulous and vague thought that there is simply something *wrong* about multinational capitalism. And this is said without being identified with a specific political ideology, which it would have been 20 years ago when the Marxist framework still prevailed. That seems to have disappeared, and what seems to have taken its place are creative forms of political invention, micro-political and macro-political invention, which seems to be rooted in forms of ethical conviction, ethical commitment. This state of affairs is something to be wished; it is also a good description of an emerging political reality. In that sense, emancipation would still be conceivable. And for me it is a question of hanging on to the notion of emancipation. Again, that's what I like in both Derrida and Habermas.

DH: And in fact you have suggested that what Derrida is attempting in his recent work is nothing less than a "repoliticization of Marxism." This led you to speculate about the potential links between deconstruction and other attempts to repoliticize Marxism. Reflecting on the Gramscian tradition that inspires Ernesto Laclau and Chantal Mouffe, you make the claim that the infinite ethical demand of deconstruction requires a theory of hegemonization.

SC: The first thing to say is about the phrase the "repoliticization of Marxism." It is a cheeky phrase because was there ever a *politicization* of Marxism? In a sense, Marx did not provide a political theory. He gave us a socioeconomic theory based upon an analysis of capital in its historical development and its actuality. Various sundry remarks about the state apparatus and perhaps unhelpful metaphors like the "base-superstructure" distinction simply make the issue worse. So in that sense what Marxism requires is a political theory. One way of re-reading Marx in that light is to look to the notion of antagonism or class struggle as being the expression of a conception of the political, or at least the possibility of a political theory. So on the one hand within Marxism there is a socioeconomic determinism and on the other hand we could say that, in key texts like the *Communist Manifesto* and the more political texts of Marx, there is the recognition that history is something that has to be constituted politically. It is not simply going to be the outcome of social and economic developments. That tradition of a political Marxism is picked up after the First World War in Italy. If the Marxism of the Second International wasn't going to produce the outcome or revolution, then politics had to be the moment that intervened into the bringing about of socialism. That is obviously the moment of Gramsci. So the politicization of Marxism happens potentially for me in Gramsci. And the central category here is the category of "hegemony," and how the left is to produce a politics that would bring about its aims, to articulate itself hegemonically because no historical theodicy is going to do the work. So what I am trying to do is to link Derrida's work (which as I see it is informed by an ethical criterion which he calls the "messianic" or "justice") with a notion of political action that I'm thinking about in relation to Laclau's notion of hegemony. What I think is lacking in Derrida is an adequate thinking of the relationship between deconstruction and hegemony, and the relationship between ethics and politics. And what I think is lacking in Laclau and Mouffe's work is an adequate thinking of the relationship between the category of hegemony and the normative basis for hegemony in some notion of ethics.

JM: In the same essay, you draw upon William Connolly's notion of deterritorialized democracy and offer some examples of new social movements like Greenpeace and Amnesty International that seem to be useful in momentarily "concretizing" Derrida's notion of "democracy to come."

SC: Bill Connolly's work interests me for all sorts of reasons, but particularly for the way in which he has tried to think the notion of democracy outside of the notion of territory. Democracy is thinkable geographically as a movement of democratization across a whole number of territorial spaces and Derrida's notion of "The New International" can be tied to such a thought of deterritorialized democratization.

DH: Elsewhere you have even proposed the marriage of Derrida and Habermas. Given the differing orientations at work in these relationships – namely, agonistic versus consensual – where do the "politics of friendship" go from here?

SC: The question of Habermas is a separate question. I spent all of 1997 and some of 1998 in Frankfurt. I went there because I was awarded a Humboldt Fellowship and because I am very curious about the Frankfurt School. I still am. One of the projects that I developed with Axel Honneth was to try to think about the possibility of a debate between a Derridean and a Habermasian paradigm. There is an interesting way of linking Derrida to Habermas and I have tried to pursue that in some of my own work. Could deconstruction provide a sort of ethical supplement to Habermasian discourse ethics? And could Habermas provide a theory of normativity that would give deconstructive ethics some grip in actual social life? So one way of pursuing the relationship between ethics and politics is in a Habermasian direction and Axel Honneth has written an article on that topic which is very interesting. But I don't think that is the most profitable way of pursuing the connection between ethics and politics. I'd pursue a much more Gramscian direction of the kind I have already sketched. However, I am interested in the conflictual space of European philosophy and how it is defined around these two gigantic figures of Derrida and Habermas. And it seems they have much more in common with each other than they imagined. In many ways, they differ most significantly on the question of politics: Habermas remains a social democrat committed to a notion of the state as a necessary horizon for political activity, whereas Derrida's ethical criterion produces a notion of democracy against the state, what he calls "democracy to come."

JM: So you now believe that the Habermasian framework can provide deconstruction with a rational procedure for legitimating and testing decisions and judgments?

SC: I think Habermas is one way of supplementing deconstruction. On my reading, Derrida's work is motivated by an ethical concern that can be understood in Levinas's sense of the word, the relation to the other. And Axel Honneth has tried to argue that Habermas's theory of justice requires, as its precondition, a notion of the ethical relation in order to be more than a mere abstraction of some sort. So the way I understand that now is, that for Honneth, Habermas's theory of justice must be connected to a conception of the good and what Levinas offers is a conception of the good, thought in terms of the ethical relation to the other. So, if – and it's a big 'if' – you can insert that conception of the good as a supplement to Habermas's theory of justice, then Honneth can claim that the goal of Habermas's discourse ethics – which is a notion of social solidarity, what he calls "the other of justice" – will be achieved. In that sense, I'm extremely sympathetic to what Honneth's up to. And for me, Derrida needs something like Habermas insofar as he needs a much more procedural notion of normativity or a theory of political action, in my terms. There is something lacking in Derrida's work. So Habermas is one way of answering that lack. It is not my preferred way of answering that lack. As I have said, I tend to deal with that in terms of Laclau's theory of hegemony. However, structurally at least, I think you can imagine an interesting marriage between Derrida and Habermas.

JM: And how do you see the terms of engagement at the moment?

SC: The terms of engagement really turn, for me, on the question of intersubjectivity. For Habermas, philosophy has to make an intersubjective turn, which it has not made in the last 200 years. Rather, it has been governed by the paradigm of individual consciousness. But intersubjectivity for Habermas is always conceived of as a relation of equality between persons who are the same. Therefore, the relation between subjects for Habermas is a relation of symmetry and reciprocity. If there is a conception of intersubjectivity in Derrida, then it is a Levinasian conception of intersubjectivity, which has to be thought of in terms of a model of asymmetry and a fundamental lack of reciprocity that defines the ethical relation. So both Derrida and Habermas are thinkers who have made the intersubjective turn but those conceptions of intersubjectivity are radically different. The way Honneth would argue it, and I tend to agree, is that if we think about intersubjectivity as equality, as a juridical or a legal relation, and we also think about intersubjectivity as asymmetry, as an ethical relation, then we have to put the ethical and the juridical together.

DH: So they can at least supplement each other around this question of intersubjectivity and justice/law and politics?

SC: Yes. The Habermasian conception of justice seems to require a notion of the good if we are not going to end up with a gap between universal pragmatics and everyday experience. This is the gap that Habermas has always wanted to bridge; in his early work, it is expressed as the relation between knowledge and human interests. On the other hand, if Derrida's conception of justice isn't simply going to remain a form of goodwill or good conscience, or a certain empty ethical universalism, then it needs to be anchored in a much more workable notion of law or politics. Again though, there may be other philosophies of law that could do that job. There is no privilege for the Habermasian one. In that respect, Derrida could be married to lots of people, not just Habermas!

JM: Your own discussions with Axel Honneth, and the role you are both playing in this debate between Derrida and Habermas, seem to suggest that there is much to be gained from keeping open a dialog between French and German contemporary philosophy.

SC: In my view, there needs to be a new approach to dialog between French and German philosophy. There is a peculiar hostility in Germany to French philosophy that has to do with the way French post-structuralism was received in Germany, that is, as a critique of what was seen as a dominant Frankfurt School or social democratic framework. For instance, Habermas says that the risk of post-structuralism is the risk of neoconservatism, which to us in the English-speaking world doesn't seem to make any sense, but it does make sense in the German context. A lot of proponents of French post-structuralism were neoconservatives. So Habermas is simply right, but we need to move beyond that.

DH: In your essay "Remarks on Derrida and Habermas" you point out that it was not until 2000 that Derrida thought it possible to have a discussion with Habermas on the question of formal pragmatics, of performativity. This is particularly interesting, given that Derrida also states that he is more and more suspicious of the theory of performativity in his written response to you.

SC: Derrida in that response makes a distinction between performativity and facticity. He argued that the emphasis or the privilege of the performative in different theoretical discourses in the West was a luxury that risked neutralizing the fact of responsibility. So he is making a distinction between performativity and facticity, where facticity is linked to responsibility. Derrida's thought is that there is an irreducible facticity to responsibility, an infinite responsibility, which is there despite me, in spite of me. So what Derrida is doing is an interesting argumentative move. He is saying we can discuss this notion of the performative but the performative has to be massively qualified; it has to be subsumed under a more radical notion of facticity, what I call in my work on Heidegger "originary facticity." And this notion of facticity produces a notion of responsibility that is overwhelming. From a Habermasian point of view, the response to this infinite responsibility is to say that it gives rise to a chronic ethical overload. This is demanding far too much of human beings, which is the way Habermas criticizes civic republicanism as a model of democracy. However, Derrida will say "well, forget that," ethics is about overload. Responsibility is either infinite or it is not responsible.

JM: Turning more closely to your work on subjectivity, why did you feel it necessary to offer a psychoanalytic account of the subject who not only experiences a Levinasian ethical relation to the other but also makes, or is made by, political decisions that take account of the third party? That is, it is the third party that is said to appear in the face of the other.

SC: Firstly, the move towards psychoanalysis is in a sense independent of my reading of Levinas. In about 1994, Peter Dews, a colleague of mine who normally taught a course on psychoanalysis, went on sabbatical. As a result, I asked, or was asked, to teach the course and became more and more convinced of psychoanalysis as a framework for thinking about philosophical issues, particularly in relation to the problematics of affectivity, desire, and sexual difference. Then, in a way, I wanted to see whether I could make sense of a thinker like Levinas in those terms. What is interesting is that Levinas has absolutely no sympathy for psychoanalysis and has only scorn for Freud's notion of the unconscious and the Lacanian notion of desire. For Levinas, it is all just pornography; he hates it. However, if Levinasian ethics and politics presuppose a notion of God, so that there is monotheism at the basis of his notion of community, and you don't want to go along with that, as I don't, then psychoanalysis can be a critical theoretical discourse for undermining that. So I am using psychoanalysis to try to think about the source of the ethical relation in ways that criticize what Levinas is explicitly up to and what a lot of his followers seem to be up to as well. So the objective of my use of psychoanalysis is to show that what is at the basis of Levinas's ethics is not a conception of God; it doesn't entail that sort of metaphysical presupposition. And furthermore, if I can make that argument, then I can show that the notion of God is not at the basis of a Levinasian politics, or a Levinasian notion of community. So for me it is terribly important to be able to redescribe the notion of the third party in Levinas – community and justice, relations between equals – in secular terms. Again that is why Habermas is interesting, because it is a rigorously secular account of community, of normativity. So that's why I made that move.

DH: You seem to have a complex, even tense, relation to Derrida's work.

SC: Absolutely. I have always been interested in making Derrida's work a lot more determinate than it wants to be. Derrida thrives on his indeterminacy. That's what is good about him, and what he teaches us is the productivity of notions of hesitation, *aporia*, undecidability, or whatever. But at a certain level that doesn't interest me; what interests me is determination, decision and coming up with a theoretical framework that can actually do something in the world.

So, to that extent, the picture that I'm offering is not really deconstructive; it is constructive. It is a construction, my construction. And in my discussions with Derrida over the years, he has been very polite and tolerant of some of the moves that I have wanted to make. Yet, it seems clear that he is involved in something that I am not really involved in. So, at that point, it is a question of just speaking for myself, philosophically, and not just doing commentary or scholarship.

DH: In that regard, you have suggested that Levinasian ethics, at least after it has been disrupted by the Derridean problem of closure, is a certain practice of language, perhaps ultimately a practice of the self in Foucault's sense. If we view Levinasian ethics as a practice of self, then might the account of "the ethical relation to the other" amount to a governing rationality of the self? That is, a governing rationality that is capable of producing a certain kind of Levinasian ethical subject rather than actually describing the ethical experience of the face-to-face?

SC: Good question. The problem of closure in Derrida's "Violence and Metaphysics" is the claim that Levinas does not adequately think through the issue of language; the ethical relation is a relationship that takes place in silence, it is a pre-linguistic relationship. Derrida rightly criticizes that. Then the reading I try to give of the later Levinas is to try to show how that notion of language becomes the basis of the ethical relationship. So, is it a practice of the self? The answer is yes. And is Levinasian ethics a practice of the self that is capable of producing a notion of the subject rather than merely describing the relationship of the face-to-face? This is where it becomes a sort of tricky question, an interesting question nonetheless. On the one hand, if Levinas is a phenomenologist then he has to be describing existing structures. The face-to-face relationship has to be something

I read off of the phenomena. This is one way of reading Levinas, particularly *Totality and Infinity*. However, it might be more persuasive to read Levinas as *exhorting* us to become selves of a certain sort. So there is a normative demand. In Foucauldian terms, there is a demand for a cultivation of the self in Levinas. That would also seem to be a strand of Levinas's work. But, if that is the case, if the ethical subject is, as it were, constituted through certain techniques, which can be cultivated, then this isn't phenomenological, it is something else. It is a technology of the self that is being described philosophically. Now, I tend towards the second position. I think that what Levinas is doing is not phenomenology in an obvious way; what he is exhorting us to do is to become subjects in a certain way. His work is marked by a more or less confused blurring of descriptive and normative claims.

DH: If so, then wouldn't this raise questions in relation to what you have claimed elsewhere regarding the distinction between the Kantian "fact of reason" and what you call Levinas's "fact of the other."

SC: It is complicated. You could say that to become a Levinasian subject is, if you like, a certain rationalization of the self that is done in relation to the fact of the other. It is not as if the fact of the other simply produces me. It isn't like I see the other suffering and I become a Levinasian. Rather, it is that there is an awareness of the other's suffering individually, globally, and then, after the fact, after the experience, it leads me to try to develop a form of subjectivity that would deal with that fact, respond to that fact, to be responsive to it. So, in that sense, you could see Levinas in much more Foucauldian terms than he is usually taken. Then the difference between Foucault and Levinas would be around the question of "what do I become a subject in the face of?" As Foucault says, in late antiquity you have techniques for becoming a self, or as it were cultivating forms of autonomy or autarchy, which are not mediated through notions of divine law in the Judaic sense or in relation to an event like the resurrected Christ. So you could say that Levinasian ethical subjectivity is a practice of the self but it is a practice of the self that would not interest Foucault because it seems to fall back into a Judeo-Christian messianism. And he is not wrong! But that doesn't mean that Foucault's position is right.

DH: How would this, if at all, connect back through to the ethical relation to the other and the decision when it comes to aesthetic judgments?

SC: Well, I am prepared to admit that maybe aesthetic judgment is like ethical judgment but I don't want to subsume ethical judgment under aesthetic judgment too readily because there are differences between artworks and human beings, even when those artworks are about human beings. There is a difference between the fact of Tricky's first album and the fact of an individual suffering. There has been a tendency in a lot of theoretical discourse to make that distinction more slippery than it needs to be. A lot of the discourse around postmodernism suffers from that fate. The other human being that suffers before me and demands my attention is not an artwork. In that sense, I would be against an ethics based upon an aesthetic cultivation. I think that leads to either a West Coast Foucauldianism or to Richard Rorty's idea of cultivating your private sphere, cultivating your sphere of private autonomy. That disgusts me. The world is full of injustice, the world is full of demands for justice and these should be rectified. These are not understandable aesthetically. People are being slaughtered in the merriest ways. Right now in Chechnya "Blood is running in the streets as if it were champagne," as Dostoyevsky would say. And that for me imposes a very clear demand, which is a normative demand, which should be met by institutional arrangements – right down to questions of international law and military intervention, for example.

2 Keep Your Mind in Hell and Despair Not

Nietzsche and the Question of Nihilism

Jill Stauffer

SAN FRANCISCO, NEW YORK, REYKJAVIK, AUGUST 2003

"Philosophy begins in disappointment" – an inversion of Aristotle's claim that philosophy begins in wonder – is perhaps Critchley's most well-known credo. In this interview, Critchley unpacks the meaning of this claim. He connects it to the basis of modern philosophical motivation, the question of nihilism, the experience of the loss of meaning, and the confrontation with finitude and death. In his second book, Very Little . . . Almost Nothing, *published in 1997, Critchley addressed these irresistible yet overpowering questions, arguing that in the wake of Nietzsche's declaration that we have murdered God, we have to cultivate alternative sources in the search for meaning – the common, the near, and the ordinary.*

In the following interview, we find an overview of these arguments. "This is the best account of what is going on in Very Little . . . Almost Nothing.*" But the discussion also leads into other kinds of responses to disappointment, which are taken up in* Infinitely Demanding. *Such responses to the contemporary crisis in meaning are wide-ranging and diverse: from Al-Qaeda's violent religious extremism to the emancipatory potential of the anti-globalization movement, and so on. The interviewer, Jill Stauffer, was at the time a PhD student at Berkeley. They met in New York and Iceland, but for the most part, that's not where the actual interview took place.*

"It was a sort of fake interview," Critchley confesses. "Jill had sent me a number of questions in writing, and I did all the answers sitting in my kitchen in Essex, speaking into a cassette recorder. I was just sitting there at the kitchen table, it was dark, and I was just speaking into one of those old-fashioned cassette recorders. I imagined she was there as I spoke."

JILL STAUFFER: You have said that philosophy begins in disappointment. What does that mean for philosophers, for human beings, for philosophy?

SIMON CRITCHLEY: There are lots of stories about how philosophy begins. Some people claim it begins in wonder; some people claim it begins in worry. I claim it begins in disappointment. And there are two forms of disappointment that interest me: religious and political disappointment. Religious disappointment flows from the realization that religious belief is not an option for us. Political disappointment flows from the fact that there is injustice – that we live in a world that is radically unjust and violent, where might seems to equal right, where the poor are exploited by the rich, etc. So for me philosophy begins with these experiences of disappointment: a disappointment at the level of what I would think of as "meaning," namely that, given that there is no God, what is the meaning of life? And, given that we live in an unjust world, how are we to bring about justice?

JS: I suspect that you will encounter little resistance with regard to the assertion that the world is unjust, but some might find the "given" that there is no God displeasing, or at least *un-*"given."

SC: Haven't you heard? God is dead.

JS: Oh, I've heard. But tell me what you mean.

31

SC: Nietzsche writes that nihilism is the experience where the highest values have devalued themselves. Where the question "why?" finds no answer. This can also be linked in Nietzsche to the problematic of the death of God. The thought in Nietzsche is not that the highest values have been devalued through some sort of general skepticism. No, Nietzsche's thought is much deeper. It is that the highest values have devalued themselves – it is a reflexive verb he uses. This is what he means by the death of God. It is not the fact that God has somehow been killed or has popped his clogs or slipped off behind the scenery, but rather that we have killed him. That's Nietzsche's full remark: "God is dead. We have killed him." The way history has worked out, Nietzsche tells us, is that the highest values in which we believed – namely, God, immortality of the soul, and whatever – have become incredible to us. We cannot believe in them. Why? Because Christianity, for Nietzsche, is driven by a will to truth. What I mean is that Christianity is not a fable for a Christian. It is not just a nice story about the creation of the world and some rabbi who got murdered by the occupying Roman authorities a couple of thousand years ago. No, for the Christian, the Christian story is true. There is a will to truth at the heart of Christianity. What the Christian realizes, in Nietzsche's account, is that the "true" world, the world of heaven, immortality, God, is untrue. It has been disproved by reason itself, by science, the will to truth. What is nihilistic for Nietzsche is the following situation: The Christian realizes that what he or she has taken to be true is in fact untrue. God is dead. And we have killed him. That drives people to declarations of meaninglessness, radical meaninglessness. It is the position that is expressed philosophically, for Nietzsche, in the work of his onetime favorite philosopher, Schopenhauer. The point of Nietzsche's work is to refuse the nihilism of the present – his late nineteenth-century present.

JS: So nihilism reigns if human beings think that there is no answer to the question of meaninglessness. And Nietzsche's point, as I see it, is that human beings are the answer. The human possibilities of thought and action defeat nihilism. If we take them on.

SC: Yes. But our present is still nihilistic. Nietzsche claimed he would be born posthumously. People are acutely aware of the meaninglessness of their existence, and they try to cover this up in a number of ways. By returning to forms of traditional religion such as fundamentalist Christianity. Or by engaging in new forms of religion – New Age belief, whether that be yoga or sitting with crystals in your hands, finding your inner child, sitting under a pyramid, or whatever. All of these are examples of passive nihilism. You might also try what Nietzsche calls active nihilism, engaging in acts of terrorism or whatever. The idea here is that, given that nothing means anything, we might as well blow the whole place up. I would recommend neither passive nor active nihilism, both of which seek to escape from the "meaning gap" in our lives. The point – the point of Nietzsche's philosophy, and of philosophy as such, in my view – is to think within that gap and work against nihilism. To use thought against the nihilism of the present.

JS: So God – or other universal or absolute ideas – cannot offer answers to the question of the meaning of life, and thus any answer has to come from within human life, which is finite and capable of error. What kind of answer can that be?

SC: Well, the answer is given in the question. The only answer to the question of the meaning of life has to begin from the fact of our human finitude, of our vulnerability and our fallibility. My personal belief that I've tried to argue for in my book *Very Little . . . Almost Nothing* – a winning title if ever there was one – is that we have to, in a sense, give up the question of the meaning of life, or at least hear it in a particular way. The formulation that I use in that book is "the acceptance of meaninglessness as the achievement of the everyday or the ordinary." What I mean by that is that once we've accepted that the meaning of life is ours to make, we make meaning. Then we accept that we live in a situation, or, rather, that we inherit a situation of meaninglessness, and out of that meaninglessness we create meaning in relationship to the ordinariness of our common existence. I try to argue for a cultivation of the low, the common and the near – the everyday – as that in relationship to which we can make a meaning out of the meaninglessness of our existence.

JS: Law is often unjust. History and the present world are full of violence and unspeakable cruelty on one hand, and mass apathy with regard to the suffering of others on the other. If we make our own meanings, that means we are entirely free not to do so. Which also means that our connection to meaning – and to ethics – is minimal, fragile, and refusable. Is there reason to hope that good can emerge out of human affairs? Where is that hope of justice and meaning that philosophy at times can provide?

SC: A huge and very difficult question. And the answer that I will give will be unsatisfactory. We have to begin from the melancholy acceptance, at least as a possibility, that perhaps nothing good comes out of human affairs. The story that I was brought up with as a kid and which was implicitly the justification for mutually assured destruction – in the nuclear standoff between the United States and the former Soviet Union – is that we had got beyond the nastiness of war. Somehow the madness of mutually assured destruction at least had the virtue of not allowing for a repeat of the Second World War. That was arguably true. But if there is a feature that dominates the present, I would say there's the fact of war, and the horror and cruelty of war. I think that the activity of thinking is and always has been, and is now increasingly, a response to political horror. We live in dark times. The people who govern us are out of touch and act in accordance with agendas that I find increasingly dispiriting. So I'm deeply pessimistic about the present situation.

JS: But you are not luxuriating in a dispirited bath of nihilism.

SC: No. Far from wanting to give up, on the contrary – this goes back to your first question – philosophy begins in the experience of political disappointment, the fact of injustice. In the face of that fact, one can create. Ethically, legally. One can try and do something. I see the work of the antiwar movement or the antiglobalization movement as huge and powerful examples of the ways in which things can be done in the face of the horror of the present. I also see these actions as processes of thought, that is, as worthy of the name "philosophy." So, although we live in dark times, and I'm pessimistic about the present situation, I'm still fantastically optimistic about what human beings can do in the face of that. But I'm talking about what human beings can do in groups, small or large, collectively. Not what governments can do. I am increasingly suspicious of the whole framework of the state and institutions such as political parties, and the whole apparatus of representative democracy, and I am more and more drawn toward more anarchistic tendencies, where politics would be focused upon the manifestation of the people against the intervention of the state. In relation to the question of hope, I think the only hope we have is hope against hope. We hope for a better world. But of course we can do better than just hope. We can act in the world. We can act ethically, we can act well. We can try to construct laws, constitutions, which are just. We can engage in political activity, and in the activity of teaching and instruction. These are tremendous activities of hope. But that's hope against hope, insofar as there is no metaphysical basis for my hope. I can't root it in religious belief. There's a lovely phrase of Gillian Rose's, which she borrowed from somebody else, which goes, "keep your mind in hell and despair not." I think of that a lot. Philosophy is keeping one's mind in hell, in the violence and cruelty of the present, and not despairing, but going on, making, creating, affirming.

JS: So if we are not to be nihilists we must recognize that philosophy is atheism, a willing embrace of a world without a higher or outside order. But somehow that doesn't consign us to a world that can only be as it is, without hope of something better.

SC: Yes. For me, there is a radical separation between philosophy – the activity of being a philosopher, someone who reflects – and a religious point of view. The philosopher is someone who doesn't know, but who wants to find out. This is why Socrates was declared the wisest man in Greece. The inscription over the oracle at Delphi reads: "Know Thyself." The truth is we do not know ourselves. The wisest of us accept that we do not know ourselves. Philosophy is the inquiry into that situation. But the religious person knows what the meaning of life is.

JS: Religion or faith is a situation into which inquiry is not necessary.

SC: Yes. The religious person knows that God is in his heaven, or that everything will turn out well in the end, or that redemption will be possible, or that if they kill themselves in a suicide-bombing incident, then they'll get to sleep with 70 virgins or whatever. I do not feel entitled to such knowledge. I suppose I still hold out the possibility of religious experience. I've just never had one. Maybe one day everything will change. I'll turn to Jesus, or Allah, or the Torah. And we'll see. But for now, in the situation I'm in at the moment, all I can do is philosophize – in the absence of anything like God. If I had a religious experience, what I know for sure is that I would stop doing philosophy and would start doing religion, teaching classes in religion, preaching in a local church. That is a fine and noble activity. But I do not feel entitled to engage in it. So for me philosophy is my fate.

JS: The philosopher doesn't "know," or she knows that she doesn't "know herself." The religious person trusts in something higher than human life, and so has a guarantee of something good in the end. So the philosopher's ethics, hopes, or values are more fragile than a religious person's. They are fragile and possibly will fail. But that is what we have if we are to change the world now instead of later. Only humans can act and change the world. But they might not do so.

SC: In your first question, you asked me what the assertion that philosophy begins in disappointment would mean for philosophers and for human beings. I want to state that, at the level of method, I don't want to make a huge distinction between philosophers and human beings. I think philosophy is the theoretical elaboration or elucidation of intuitions that are common to human beings. Philosophy just makes that manifest through a certain discipline of reflection. So philosophy, for me, is a way of relearning to look at the world, a world that is familiar to us, that we know, that is shared by all human beings and also by nonhuman beings. I think that when people are at their best, when they are thinking, reflecting, cogitating, then they are doing philosophy. So I don't see philosophy as an academic enterprise. If I did, I think I'd slit my wrists and go sit in a bath and die like a good Roman. For me, philosophy is an activity of thought that is common to human beings. Human beings at their best. Or, to use the phrase of Stanley Cavell, "Philosophy is the education of grown-ups."

JS: The points about resisting nihilism and being grown-up seem to have something to do with what it means to live in a secular society, or in a society that can't be ordered by belief in one idea, God, or order.

SC: That's absolutely right. There's a lot of debate about secularism among people who claim that we can no longer accept that we live in a secularist world – by people as clever as William Connolly, whose last book was called *Why I Am Not a Secularist*. One of the intellectual tendencies at present is a massive return to religion, usually in the guise of postmodernism. I think this is lamentable. To be honest I think it's a little disgusting. Not that Connolly is disgusting, of course.

JS: Connolly's book seems to me to be about how to be a good secularist instead of a bad one. At least, according to his definitions. But what is religion in the guise of postmodernism?

SC: The problem of secularism, the problem of the secular world, is that we haven't achieved it yet. In my view, the problem of modernity is not that we have somehow got beyond modernity into postmodernity. On the contrary, we haven't achieved modernity. Modernity would be the achievement of a secular form of life, and we haven't got there yet. This is a position that I owe to my great friend Jay Bernstein. The philosophical task – and also the political, ethical, legal task – is the achievement of a secular society.

If we think about something like the war in Iraq, it was an entirely religious war. And it does indeed correspond to a reactionary right-wing diagnosis of the present, such as that of Samuel Huntington (*The Clash of Civilizations and the Remaking of World Order*). The US–Iraq conflict is a confrontation between two versions of religious metaphysics. That is what we have to get rid of. People are perfectly happy to reject the terrorist metaphysics of Al-Qaeda, but they should be equally active in rejecting the reactive metaphysics of George W. Bush, which has transformed political discourse into religious discourse – in particular through his careless use of categories such as "evil."

JS: If there is no final authority that stands higher than what human beings create, how can we know what right and wrong are? What stability can categories of reason have? And what place can justice or ethics have in such a scheme?

SC: These are important questions. I think you are asking after a form of authority, which is simply not available to us. If there is no higher authority than what human hands, brains, and bodies are able to create, then right and wrong are what we declare to be right and wrong. Ethics, justice, and law are not handed to us on Sinai on large tablets; they are things that we have to create for ourselves. We have to become grown-ups. The problem that is raised – the deep problem that is raised by your question – is what justification is there for one conception of right and wrong over another conception of right and wrong? The problem that giving up religious belief creates is the problem of moral skepticism: I say good, you say bad . . . or you say good, I say bad, virtue and vice spin and turn, moral language becomes increasingly ambiguous. How do we arrest that? Well, there are various means. Some people will want to base right and wrong in the life of a specific community, which could be relatively large, like a nation-state, or it could be very small, as small as a monastery or a school. Other people will want to base right and wrong in a procedure of what philosophers call universalization, namely that the only norms we can act on justly are ones that all human beings could justifiably act on. And so on and so forth. Contemporary moral theory, dominated by the three standard theories of justification – deontology, consequentialism, and virtue ethics – is born out of the recognition that this is our situation. Now, my present work is on ethics, and I am trying to answer this question. I think that one has to recognize that there is a point at which moral argumentation breaks down. I'm calling my next book *Ethics . . . My Way*. [Editor's note: This book was later titled *Infinitely Demanding*.] And implicit within such a title is acceptance of the fact that I can try to produce as rational and coherent a theory of ethics as is possible, but in a sense I'm not going to be able to convince the skeptic. There's a point where moral argumentation reaches a limit. What I can do is recommend a certain view to you in the most persuasive terms and hope that you accept it.

JS: Would you like to say more to recommend your view?

SC: The book on ethics is really a book against ethics, or against the way ethics is commonly talked about in universities. I think that ethics has become too focused on questions of justification; how we justify different norms of action, whether we do that by universalizing them if we're a Kantian; or referring them to the greatest happiness, the greatest number, if we're a Utilitarian; or referring them to the virtues of a specific community if we are a neo-Aristotelian. I think this risks reducing morality to a sort of student party game that is at its most extreme in certain tendencies in applied ethics: "Hands up who thinks we should switch off the life-support machine!" Though there are also some better tendencies in applied ethics. For me, the issue is not so much justification as motivation, that in virtue of which a self can be motivated to act on some conception of the good.

JS: You want to focus on an individual's commitment to ethics or to the good, whatever that might be, instead of beginning with the search for justification.

SC: Yes. That requires some sort of account of what we might call the existential matrix of ethics. So, for me, the basic question of ethics is: How does a self bind itself to whatever it determines as its good? And in order to answer that question I think we need a description and an explanation of the deep subjective commitment to ethical action, of what it really feels like for a self to be faithful to its beliefs. Commitment, which is a nicely old-fashioned and discredited concept, interests me greatly. So, *Ethics . . . My Way* is basically an argument for the committed ethical subject that explains why it is that we act morally. My core claim is that the ethical subject takes shape in relation to a felt demand, a demand that can take various forms. On my version of ethics, the subject is committed to a demand which is unfulfillable, one-sided, and radical; this is the demand that is felt in the presence of the other person, neighbor, or stranger, what Emmanuel Levinas calls "the face."

JS: This will sound metaphysical to many, but for Levinas it is the most concrete demand. How else could I feel distress at harm that others undergo but which I have done nothing to cause? An ethical commitment affects me prior to my ability to decide to take it on.

SC: Right. The face of the other makes an overwhelming demand upon me, which I can never hope to meet but which prompts my ethical action in the world. In my view, ethical action is taken in the face of infinite responsibility, a responsibility that I can never fully discharge, a responsibility that pushes me on to try to do more, not just for this particular other in front of me, but for all others in the world.

JS: That challenges conceptions that would claim that we have duties only if we consent to give up freedoms: "If I owe something to you, it is because I choose to." But what you're describing is a weightier demand. It can be ignored, but it cannot be willed away – it isn't subject to will or is prior to any possibility of willing.

SC: Ethics is a heavy load and it is always already political; it is always taken in a context where one is endlessly compromised in a play of struggle and power, what Gramsci called "hegemony." At the end of the book, which I have not written yet because it is such a difficult topic, I try to broach the question of the relation between ethical action and politics. I will let you know how it turns out.

JS: I think most people think that reason and its categories are what rescue us from the blindness or irrationality of faith. But what you've been saying reminds us that such a belief – belief in the effectiveness and reliability of reason – is itself a faith, a faith in reason. Such a faith hasn't let go of the need for faith in something with a final authority outside of human hands.

SC: It's a good point. And it is one that we must borrow again from Nietzsche. I should say that Nietzsche isn't my favorite philosopher. But I think he is powerful and incontrovertible in all sorts of ways. The point about reason in Nietzsche is that faith in the categories of reason is, as he says, the cause of nihilism. This could be linked to a thought inherited from Nietzsche through the work of Max Weber into the thought of the Frankfurt School, in particular Adorno and

Horkheimer's *Dialectic of Enlightenment*. The thought here is that reason, which was that in which we had faith in the period of the Enlightenment – the eighteenth century – has undergone a reversal, an inversion, a dialectical transformation. The reason that was meant to be our salvation – to be, in Kant's words, man's freedom from his self-incurred tutelage – has become the means of our imprisonment. It has become the instrumental rationality, the bureaucratic rationality, that governs contemporary society. This is the version of rationality that was also discussed by Foucault in his idea that we live in societies of surveillance, discipline, and control.

JS: Turns out, reason has not set us free.

SC: The point is not to abandon reason, but to face up to what reason has become for us, and to imagine both new forms of rationality – more capacious forms of rationality that would be capable of acknowledging the experience of communication, of dependence, of vulnerability. That is, of imagining emancipatory forms of reason. That's not something that my work is particularly devoted to, but I think it's a noble task, something we ought to take seriously. This would be an experience of reason where the opposition between reason and faith would begin to fall apart. A more capacious notion of reason would carry within it that stratum of experience that we normally associate with faith, the life of the passions, the affective emotional life, and so on and so forth.

JS: Well, if the aim of such a rationality is to become capable of acknowledging the experiences of communication, vulnerability, and dependence, that seems to me to be very much related to your concern that ethics always ought to refer back to the ethical subject rather than jumping straight onto the bandwagon of universality or utility.

Communication, vulnerability, and dependence (and their various failures) often wake us, at times forcefully, from the dream of universality. And a more capacious kind of reason, I would hazard, would make us re-view the world, perhaps phenomenologically. Should we talk about phenomenology and its possible relation to ethics?

SC: If you say so. Merleau-Ponty says that true philosophy consists in relearning to look at the world. Philosophy teaches us to look at the world again. It brings out at a theoretical level what all plain, common, ordinary people, in a sense, know already. That's also a definition of phenomenology. Another formulation of the term would be to say that phenomenology is the unveiling of the pre-theoretical layer of human experience. We exist in a world; we exist practically in an everyday manner. Phenomenology is a philosophical method that tries to uncover that pre-theoretical layer of human experience and redescribe it. That, in a sense, sounds a little obscure and uninteresting. I'd sharpen it up by thinking about the relation between phenomenology and the scientific worldview. We live in a world that is dominated by science. And that's not a bad thing – not at all. But one of the problems with the scientific worldview is that it leads human beings to have an overwhelmingly theoretical relationship to the world. For example, I no longer accept my being in the world practically and then try to describe that or elucidate that; rather, I see the world theoretically as colors and objects and representations, which are fed through my retina into the brain.

JS: The theoretical version gets prioritized.

SC: Right. Then one can ask all sorts of neurophysiological questions about the nature of the brain, the nature of perception, and so on and so forth. That is important stuff. But what I want to stay with philosophically, and what phenomenology gives to us, is a sense of the obvious – that which is in front of our eyes, the below, the near, the common – I want to try to elucidate that. So phenomenology is a relearning of how we see the world in its presence, its palpable and practical presence.

JS: So the obvious is actually not so obvious. We don't see it until we learn to look. Or what is nearest to us is often what is furthest from us in terms of our thinking, as Heidegger might say. Could we say that the difference between the scientific and phenomenological views is the difference between a theory of the world and an experience of the world?

SC: Well, phenomenology is not an empiricism. Empiricism would be another version of theory that phenomenology would want to reject. Phenomenology is about the uncovering of a layer of acquaintance with the world that we know but that, in a sense, we conceal through our scientific and theoretical activity.

JS: Right. We conceal the obvious in order to lay stress on other things. Could we say phenomenology is a living knowledge of the world?

SC: I think I would say that phenomenology is the power of reflection brought to bear on the fact of being-in-the-world.

JS: Philosophy begins in disappointment. Does philosophy end, and if so, how?

SC: Well, as I've already admitted, philosophy could end for me if I underwent a religious experience or became an anti-intellectual philistine. Perhaps those two alternatives would amount to the same conclusion. But, on the contrary: For me, philosophy does not end. I disagree, therefore, vehemently with someone like Richard Rorty who would see the whole activity of philosophy as something we can consign to the past, so that we should engage ourselves in literary criticism, the writing of history and politics, instead of philosophy. Here, of course, Rorty follows David Hume. On the contrary. For me, because of the fact of something like political horror, because of the fact that the question of meaning still eats away at us, we require philosophy as a means of reflection and thought, which aims toward emancipating human beings from situations of unfreedom and pushing them toward the possibility of freedom.

JS: And it all comes down to us: human beings. We're the cause of political horror, but also the possibility of its solution or end. And we're also the only ones capable of creating meaning or further possibility for ourselves and others. Philosophy is the pursuit of possibility.

SC: Philosophy isn't programmed into us, and a lot of the forces of our culture steadfastly work against it. Philosophy, for me, is a way of resisting the nihilism of the present by making, creating, affirming. By going on. In many ways, the philosophical motto here could be taken from someone like Samuel Beckett: "I can't go on; I'll go on." Or, as Pascal says (and this is a phrase that lives with me all the time), "Man is a reed, the weakest in nature; a virus, a vapor is enough to kill him. But man can think. And it is in this that our dignity consists. Let us strive to think well." Philosophy is this striving to think well. To give that up would be to give up the most sizable portion of our humanity.

This interview appeared originally in the May 2003
issue of *The Believer Magazine*.

3 The State is a Limitation on Human Existence

Gramsci and Hegemony

Gijs Van Oenen, Irena Rosenthal, and Ruth Sonderegger

AMSTERDAM, JUNE 2008

This interview for Krisis: Journal of Contemporary Philosophy *continues to investigate the theme of politics. It was conducted in the summer of 2008, about a year after the publication of* Infinitely Demanding, *and is mainly concerned with the arguments posed there. While relatively short, this book offers a comprehensive yet detailed account of Critchley's political position, firmly situated in the context of contemporary political thought, with engaging commentaries on Rancière, Negri, Habermas, and Badiou. The guiding question, both for the book and the interview, is the following: In a time where the political left is suffering from an impotence of imagination, what new forms of political organization have emerged, or might emerge in the future? In his response, Critchley emphasizes the successful mobilization of political anger that he sees embodied in contemporary neo-anarchist movements. To this end, he turns to Gramsci and his theory of hegemony, especially the way this theory is extended in the work of Laclau. "Gramsci was really important to me. My relation to Gramsci was through Laclau, insofar as we were trying to work out what Laclau was saying. I learned to think about politics through Laclau, rather than just sentimentalizing about politics." Of the actual interview, Critchley seems to remember very little . . . almost nothing. "It took place in a tiny little office in*

47

the philosophy department at the University of Amsterdam, on the Nieuwe Doelenstraat. I remember it was very hot and I was sweating profusely, but that's about it."

KRISIS: The main problem that you address in *Infinitely Demanding* is a so-called "motivational deficit in liberal democracy." We have two questions with regard to your analysis of the motivational deficit. First, to what extent is there such a motivational deficit? You emphasize all sorts of informal local activities. Does this not suggest that there is a lot of motivation, interest, and willingness to engage in political action? Is the problem of motivation then not a purely philosophical, Kantian problem that has disappeared on the local level of secular liberal democracies at least?

Secondly, you conceptualize the motivational deficit in distinctly ethical terms. Yet your main target is political: you criticize a particular conception of political life or political conviction, namely, the Bush administration. To what extent is your ethical interpretation of the motivational deficit adequate to address the political problems you identify? Put otherwise: How should we see the relation between the motivational deficit and the war on terror?

SIMON CRITCHLEY: The main claim I make is that there is a motivational deficit in secular liberal democracy, in its institutions, its habits. This is the problem or crisis in normal politics: a demotivation in multi-party politics and parliamentary politics. On the other hand, there is a remotivation at the level of non-governmental or non-parliamentary politics. New forms of politics have emerged – forms that I call "neo-anarchist" – that are successfully mobilizing existing political anger that no longer resonates with classical forms of politics.

The motivational deficit in liberal democracy in relation to the Bush regime is complicated. There is not a necessary link between the two but we should note that the Bush regime has a lot of motivational power. It is a theological project: even though it makes noises of the secular type – say on human rights – it is doing politics through right-wing evangelism. That is one way of doing politics. I don't think that it is the best way of doing it; it is the response on the left that interests me. The Bush regime understands the nature of politics or how popular fronts can be formed. They are good students of Carl Schmitt and even Gramsci. They understand how coalitions are built. With the Bush regime, you know what you get: a clear Straussian agenda. There is an intellectual dignity to the project whatever you think of it. Left liberals in the US on the other hand have been clueless for 30 years. The opposition on the left is either sentimental or constitutional. Look at where all the American Habermasians have ended up: all they think of is law, legal issues, constitutional niceties. To that extent, I am much more critical of the Democratic Party and the left liberals than I am of the Bush regime.

KR: But has liberal democracy not been successful up to a certain degree? Of course, not everyone is included, but there has been a practical learning process in liberal-democratic states.

SC: One possibility is to stay in the framework of liberal democracy and try to defend it against conservative undermining, and improve it. That is a good Habermasian response. I don't believe in it for a moment. I don't think there was an "Enlightenment project," as Habermas put it. In fact, I think that this is a weird version of history. It made sense as a response to the disaster of National Socialism, the need to engage in a *Normalisierung* of German philosophy and German politics. To that extent it has been successful. But elsewhere? Motivations are so much more complicated than Enlightenment norms; think of the strength of national, religious, and ethnic affiliations.

KR: But once you reject that liberal democracy has been successful or has a potential for improvement, do you not end up with the old-fashioned idea of politics as directed against the state? Is *real* politics non-governmental, anti-institutional or anti-state politics? Should we forget about the state and institutions? Or is the problem or challenge rather that of linking institutional and legal politics with new forms of politics?

SC: The last option. But I begin with the ontological premise that the state is a limitation on human existence. I am against the state, law, bureaucracy, and capital. I see anarchism as the only desirable way of organizing politically. I have always been very suspicious of authoritarian forms of Marxism and crypto-authoritarian forms of Marxism in different guises. Anarchism for me is a practice of popular self-determination and its political form is federalist. I can imagine a series of moves that could be made to establish a radically federalist form of politics in, for example, Western Europe. You just decide to abolish all the nationalist state structures and have the EU or some loose framework in which there is local autonomy on the level of towns or regions. It would be like Gandhi's vision of India as consisting of a 100,000 self-governing villages. There is just not a will to do it, certainly not in established politics, because politicians would vote themselves out of existence. In my view, anarchism is not that unrealistic: it is a way of describing how people actually organize practically, doing things in localities all over the place. Its power is on the practical level; its weakness is theoretical. Anarchists are good at practice but not in theory; that is why the universities are full of Marxists. Marxism works perfectly in the university machine. But if you push anarchists theoretically, it is often not very interesting. "Too much apple pie," as I put it in my book *Infinitely Demanding*.

KR: Can we give you a Gramscian counterexample? Gramsci talked to laborers in factories trying to get them organized in an anarchist way, but he was resented by both laborers and the labor unions for disrupting and undermining the fragile bonds of labor solidarity that had been precariously established. More generally, it is very unattractive to get organized in something like a *Räterepublik* because it is unclear what it has to offer and tends to be very unstable.

SC: The problem is that people have been ideologically cultivated to identify with the nation-state and its institutions. It is seemingly terrifying to think of an alternative to the nation-state. And although I have worked as a union activist, unions are not always the best allies: as we can see in the history of unions in the US, union activities can be very reactionary and conservative.

Now, to go back to the question of the state: I don't think a society without the state is the only desirable outcome in politics. As Schmitt said, there are two traditions in political thought: authoritarian and anarchist. They both derive from conceptions of human nature. If you think human beings are wicked, you turn to an authoritarian conception of politics, the Hobbesian–Machiavellian–Straussian line. That will always be more attractive to intellectuals because they think of themselves as having deeper insight into human nature and it corresponds to the wickedness we intellectuals tend to see all over the place. You then end up with a leftist Schmittianism, such as defended by Chantal Mouffe, who presents a Freudian anthropology that focuses on the wickedness of human beings. That is a convenient and easy position to defend because you will never be contradicted by events. Anarchism, in contrast, is based upon a certain innocence and optimism about human nature, or better, about human capacities. In that sense, I am a utopian and an optimist about what human beings are capable of and I look for that evidence or examples as to how human beings will freely and mutually cooperate outside the activities of the state.

Now, the question of linking new forms of politics and institutions has indeed become crucial. The sequence of politics from, say, 1999 to the antiwar demonstrations and the rest is in many ways encountering the limits of the politics of protest. In the final chapter of *Infinitely Demanding*, I defend politics as the creation of "interstitial distance" within the state.

What I am interested in is how new forms of political subjectivity are formed and created, how new spaces are opened, just like the politics of sexuality in the past couple of generations. This does not proceed at a distance from the state but tries to force a space within the state. I have just spent ten days at home in England. Very depressing. The state saturates all areas of social life through surveillance to a degree that would have been unimaginable 20 years ago. It shocked me. If you cross London, you are photographed 30 times. There is thus no space in the state and politics consists in the creation of such a space around a demand and then articulating it in relation to the state. In the book, I illustrate this with the indigenous rights movement in Mexico from the 1980s to the present. The classical category of resistance in Mexican politics, the peasant, had ceased to be effective. But there was the possibility of the creation of a new political subject, the indigenous, at a distance from the state. This happened by using the lever of the right to create that distance. Rights are levers of political articulation.

My concept of politics thus differs from a theorist like Rancière, who is after a more ethics-free conception of politics. Rancière's concept of politics is descriptively powerful for certain situations, such as the protests against the French in Algeria, which for him is a paradigmatic case. But politics for him is a spontaneous emergence of *la politique*; there is no normative framework or notion of ethical subjectivity around which you can build such a notion of politics. For him, that would be just another symptom of nihilism. Mouffe, on the other hand, wants a Schmittianism without Catholicism, which is completely implausible because Catholicism is what is doing the motivational work for Schmitt.

KR: You strongly emphasize that new forms of political subjectivity need to be theorized in an ethical vocabulary rather than in purely political terms. With regard to the linkage between ontology and politics, you take a radically different stance. For instance, you reject a conceptualization of an ontology of the social in favor of purely political terms. Is that not a dangerous strategy, given the current political predicament? Both individualist right-based conceptions of state-centered liberalism, as well as strong conceptions of community as defended by, say, the teleological civilizationists and neo-Schmittians, lay a claim on social life. Resistance against these hegemonic projects, as Gramsci suggested, proceeds through coalitions that need some sort of practice-based action, such as habits and rituals. Do philosophers not have a role in cultivating some ontological premises that bring to light a conception of social practice that is neither individualist nor communitarian? Is an ontology-free conception of politics not overly vulnerable?

SC: Yes, such a conception is vulnerable. There is no ontology that can be appealed to as a basis for organizing political life, whether that is Negri's idea of the multitude or Habermas's idea of communicative rationality. I reject the search for guarantees or deeper structures that underlie political activities. This is why I am interested in a philosopher like Badiou: he makes the ontological question as uninteresting as possible. The ontological questions are just explained by set theory because for him that is the best language we have to express being qua being. Regardless of whether that is true or not, the consequence of that is a radical deflation of the ontological question. For Badiou, the philosophical question is not about producing events but about describing the conditions under which events have happened or might happen. I find that much more appealing: There is no transitivity between ontology and politics.

I am arguing against strong ontological readings of Marx that are based on his idea of species-being (*Gattungswesen*) but particularly against Hardt and Negri. For a Spinozist like Negri, there is one substance: nature or the multitude. The present condition is under the reign of empire but it will shift to multitude. There is of course a change of the modality of the substance, but the ontology is doing the work. I am as suspicious of that as I am of the ontologization of politics in Heidegger. Heidegger's idea is that if you get the fundamental ontology in place, this can then be elaborated on the level of political engagement. That is what he did in 1933 and that partly explains why I argue for a separation between politics and ontology. Politics is about politics. Gramsci understood that: politics is about forging coalitions and there is no support on the ontological level or logic of history that is going to do anything. Even though Badiou is not a reader of Gramsci, you find this in Badiou as well: events are constructed by the people without an ontological support. Such is my position. Now, I am in the process of qualifying this a bit: the construction of such events could be called ontological. Badiou and I had a debate about this very issue which is available online. But I am now prepared to concede that the creation of political subjectivity is about the ontology of the new and you could give a Foucauldian twist to that if that turns you on.

KR: So you are in between pure spontaneous happenings, as argued for by Rancière, and stable ontologies. Is this why you emphasize the ethical moment, because it gives some stability and does not leave everything to chance?

SC: I don't use the word stable. You often hear theorists say that true politics is rare. That is a Heideggerian trope, which we can do without. That is just not true sociologically speaking; there are all sorts of things happening. And people are doing these things not on the basis of purely political imperatives but usually on the basis of ideas of responsibility, responding to certain wrongs and injustice in mainly ethical frameworks. The theoretical task is complicated: on the one hand, I want to describe things that are actually happening but, on the other hand, I give a normative recommendation. My belief about ethics is that it is in the business of giving recommendations and nothing more. Ethics is not like logic that is true in virtue of its form or natural science that is true in virtue of its verified validity. Normative considerations are true in virtue of being recommended and accepted as such. Nothing is doing the work behind our back; once again, that is my worry about Habermasian approaches. Furthermore, if ethics would give more than recommendations it would be against a conception of freedom: you cannot force people to be free as Rousseau wished. Therefore, I am trying to give a picture of ethical subjectivity drawing on Lacan, Badiou, and Løgstrup. It is perhaps an overly philosophical image but what it comes down to for me is anarchism. Today, on the way in from Amsterdam's central station, I saw an anarchist slogan on the wall: "Freedom lives when the state dies." That is the classical anarchist position. I am arguing for an anarchism of responsibility, a Levinasian anarchism. Anarchism in the 1960s was libertarian and organized around issues of sexual liberation. That moment has passed. People are and should be organizing around responsibility.

KR: Let us go back to Gramsci again. During the 1970s, many people found Gramsci liberating because of his emphasis on the importance of civil society as against the omnipresent state. Do you believe in the existence of a civil society?

Let us specify this question with an example. There was a big research project done in the Netherlands on state initiatives with regard to the integration of minorities. The result of this project showed that integration was largely successful but integration policy was mainly unsuccessful. This suggests that there is something like a civil society, which has some authority over individuals and acts behind our backs.

SC: Yes, there is a civil society and Gramsci was very eloquent in describing it. The difficulty is that civil society can also yield forms of authoritarianism: it depends on the context. Take integration. One image of England is based around the notion of the integrated commercial city with London as a paradigm case. You can imagine describing that like Homi Bhabha does: putting emphasis on the emergence of hybrid cultures. I sometimes believe that. But then you have 7/7, the so-called terrorist attacks in London by second-generation working-class Muslims from the depressed north of England. This leads to a different picture of civil society which puts more stress on exclusion. Yet I remain essentially positive about civil society. There is something endlessly creative and fascinating to it. Not for nothing, I am currently writing a book on Rousseau which circles around the catechism of citizenship. [Editor's note: This book will appear in 2012 under the title *The Faith of the Faithless*.]

KR: By way of conclusion, could you elaborate on this catechism a bit? How far does your new book on citizenship differ from the political ethics you developed in *Infinitely Demanding*?

SC: It is an attempt to develop the position in *Infinitely Demanding* into questions about the relation between three concepts: politics, law, and religion. A version comes out in German in September with *Diaphanes*, though I am still working on the argument. Very simply, this research is about the relation between politics and belief. I argue that there is no politics worthy of the name without the experience of something like belief. As Oscar Wilde says, "Every thing to be true must become a religion." I try to show the necessity for a moment of sacralization in the constitution of any polity and lay out a history of such sacralization, with historical examples of civil religion from the ancient Greeks through to American democracy, state socialism, current – often vacuous – debates about European identity, and the specter of Jihadism. Using Rousseau as a guide, I will show in detail how politics and law require something like religion to bind citizens together. This is what I call "the catechism of the citizen." Such a model of politics significantly challenges the standard left-liberal secularization narrative. I conclude by criticizing the contemporary theologization of politics, arguing instead for belief at the level of poetry rather than religion. This leads to the closing hypothesis of what I call "a politics of the supreme fiction," where I try to draw together my work on poetry – particularly Wallace Stevens, whose work I have been engaged with for years – with my interest in politics. To be honest, I am not sure at this stage if my argument is plausible. I am going to try to work it out in my teaching this autumn.

This interview was originally published in *Krisis: Journal for Contemporary Philosophy* 2, 2008.

4 Infinitely Demanding Anarchism

Marxism and the Political

Seferin James

DUBLIN, HOWIE-IN-THE-HILLS, FL, MARCH 2009

This interview picks up on and extends themes discussed in the first and third interviews: the ethical reading of Derrida's thought and its political consequences, and the possibilities of emerging forms of politics. We find here a detailed account of Critchley's engagement with anarchism, as expressed in Infinitely Demanding. *A crucial question for Critchley is how Marxist conceptions of the political can be revived in the context of anarchism. Central to this task is a discussion of the role of the state. For Critchley, the state is here to stay. Yet anarchism can lead to the re-articulation of political projects by turning the state into a "radical form of federalism." In an attempt to bridge the gap between ethical and political interests, Critchley supplements his anarchist politics with a description of the ethical structure operative in any political subjectivity: that of the political demand.*

In contrast to the other interviews in this collection, Critchley had never met or spoken with this interrogator previously. "This was done over the phone when I was in Florida. I think the result was pretty good, which is surprising because it was a phone interview with a complete stranger, and phone interviews are usually rather terrible!" The strangeness was multiplied by a certain mise-en-scène. "My wife, her father, and my stepson had all gone to Disneyworld and I was sitting there in a town called Howie-in-the-Hills, wearing a dressing gown I'd just bought from Target, staring at a golf course."

58

SEFERIN JAMES: Your landmark work, *The Ethics of Deconstruction*, faced the difficult task of coming to terms with the ethical significance of Jacques Derrida's work. With your more recent book, *Infinitely Demanding*, you continue to work with ethical insights derived from Emmanuel Levinas but the only reference to Derrida is a single footnote. In your 2008 paper "Derrida the Reader," you discuss some of your reservations about Derrida's philosophy, including the debate over the term "post-structuralism" and the popular idea of deconstruction. If you have substantially abandoned Derrida's philosophy, could you shed some light on what has motivated this departure?

SIMON CRITCHLEY: I've had this question before. It's a difficult one to answer because, for me, Derrida was *the* philosopher. I was educated in England in the 1980s and in France in a very Heideggerian context. When the question of Heidegger's politics really came up, which was in 1987, I was just a first-year graduate student. It was a revelation. There were things that we didn't really know, things that we hadn't been told. The attack on Heidegger was ferocious but it's difficult to reconstruct that context. The best way of getting at it is in Badiou's *Manifesto for Philosophy*, where he spends the first five or six chapters attacking a sort of Heideggerian orthodoxy. I taught that text last year and students don't really see that because it doesn't really exist in at all the same way now. It really was the case that every major thinker was a modulation or modification of what Heidegger was up to – a different way of hearing it, and in particular Derrida. The attack on Heidegger and Heidegger's politics in 1987, centered around the book by Farías, raised this issue of ethics in a particularly powerful way. That sort of got me into this topic of ethics at a very early level. There seemed to be no ethical resources in Heidegger's thought for resisting National Socialism.

SJ: So it was the question over Heidegger's politics that gave you an impetus towards ethics as a primary concern in your philosophy?

SC: I had different PhD projects. One of the first projects was going to be on the idea of memory in Hegel, which at some point I will go back to. Another was on Husserl; I was looking into the nature of transcendental argumentation in Derrida and Husserl and I just decided that I couldn't really organize the material. Then this issue of Heidegger's politics exploded and the figure that everyone who had taught me seemed to revere, seemed to have, if not blood on his hands, at least the stains of something unpleasant on his clothes in the closet. I'd read Levinas before, quite carefully, in another context. I read all that in French because he wasn't really available in translation, and I began to try to formulate a response to that.

Derrida was very much the philosophical avant-garde, the highest expression of the philosophical avant-garde in that period. The text of his that was really very important to me was *Of Spirit, De l'Esprit*, where he responds to, and with, Heidegger. He implicitly responds to the issue of politics and to the fact that the attack on Heidegger was implicitly an attack on Derrida, which is how it was: it was an attack on deconstruction. He formulated this idea of the pledge and of responsibility and the rest. I've always seen Derrida's thought as shifting between two poles, a Heideggerian pole and a Levinasian pole, and it shifts much more closely to the Levinasian pole after the political debacle of 1986–7. As Derrida was *the* philosopher, the philosopher's philosopher, in the sense that he was someone that people interested in philosophy were watching, there was a question of defending him at a certain level and trying to clarify what I saw as the basic gesture of his thinking – which had this ethical orientation. Now that seems entirely banal. It's peculiar the way history works. There's a sort of vague consensus that there was a shift in Derrida's work in that period, but it wasn't evident at the time. But there are people who accept that and there are also people who don't accept it, like Martin Hägglund. In any case, it required an enormous amount of work to excavate that. There was an enormous initial skepticism, which is something that had always been on my mind.

The question you ask is why that is mostly absent from *Infinitely Demanding*. The answer is, I don't really know. It's peculiar the way Derrida dropped from my attention at a certain point and I don't fully understand why that happened. Partly it has to do with a sort of frustration that I think I felt and a lot of people felt with what was happening with his thought in the 1990s. It seemed to be the wrong discourse. The last time I really taught Derrida at Essex was *Politics of Friendship* and *Specters of Marx* and it seemed somehow irrelevant to the students I was teaching it to, and this really struck me. It was maybe the wrong moment for Derrida's work, that scrupulousness and care and patience and whatever just seemed to be suddenly irrelevant. The time required something different, and there was an enormous impatience with that scrupulousness. I suppose some of that impatience infected me. I wrote something after his death but in the last ten or fifteen years I haven't been engaged with Derrida in the way in which I was.

SJ: Would you like to comment on your general relationship to phenomenology at the moment?

SC: I still think of myself as a phenomenologist. I'm teaching *Being and Time* for 14 weeks this semester. It is the sort of thing that you can do here in the USA that you can't do with the English term system where you are teaching nine-week courses and it tends to be very superficial. We're really going through the text very carefully for the next 14 weeks and it

reminds me how committed I am to Heidegger's conception of phenomenology. I try to show in the book that came
out last year, *On Heidegger's Being and Time*, that Heidegger's
conception of phenomenology is really derived from a
certain reading of Husserl, with other things added in along
the way. I try to show how Heidegger's phenomenology is a
radicalization of things that are already there in Husserl. You
can say that it is all in Husserl but it is Heidegger that synthe-
sizes those things into a new chemistry, blending them with
elements from Dilthey, and a certain reading of Aristotle, and
a certain Christian – radical Christian – orientation: Paul,
Augustine, and Luther.

Heidegger's conception of phenomenology, which is this
idea of attempting, through philosophical discourse, to get
close to that which shows itself; and language is that power
of articulation, that power of intelligibility, which allows you
to attend to that which shows itself. How Heidegger defines
the phenomenon is something that I still relish and subscribe
to. The issue then is whether accepting that means subscrib-
ing to the sort of narrative of Heidegger's work in *Being and
Time* as he describes it.

Levinas says that the task is leaving the climate of
Heidegger's thinking without leaving for a climate that
would be pre-Heideggerian. That's very much how I situate
what I'm up to. I think that there are problems with the
climate or the ethos of Heidegger's work, particularly around
the question of authenticity for me, but there is no step back
behind Heidegger to some pre-Heideggerian metaphysics or
whatever. The step that Heidegger makes is a decisive step;
therefore it's a question of how one negotiates philosophically on the ground laid out by Heidegger, using different
emphases than the ones that Heidegger himself gave. So I
think it's a question of reading *Being and Time*, and also much
of the later work, with Heidegger against Heidegger. That's
nothing new; Habermas's first published paper was called

"With Heidegger, Against Heidegger," as I recall, which is a reading of the 1935 *Introduction to Metaphysics*, published in 1953 So I still think of myself as a phenomenologist because for me the overwhelming threat or worry is the worry of what Husserl called objectivism, what we call now naturalism or scientism. Phenomenology still has a lot to offer and I subscribe wholeheartedly to that.

SJ: It's very interesting, the narrative that you suggest. You begin with the question that Heidegger's politics casts over his philosophy. This leads you to your PhD thesis *The Ethics of Deconstruction*, which considers the ethical resources available through Levinas to a Heideggerian tradition of thought. Then in your recent work, *Infinitely Demanding*, you seem to continue this trajectory inspired by the question of fascism towards a kind of pacifist anarchism.

SC: A bit of background here is that my political trajectory has been through a number of changes in the last ten or fifteen years. To a great extent, this has been dependent on what has been going on in the outside world and also who I'm talking to. What you find in *Infinitely Demanding* is that I begin with this engagement with Marx that comes out of a whole series of encounters I was having – reading groups in 2000 and 2001, where people wanted to go back to Marx. I've got an implicit trust in what people are interested in. I tend to listen very carefully to what graduate students are talking about and reading. The reading of Marx really came out of a long-term engagement I've had with Marx, but also out of a sense of urgency – an urgency to go back to Marx and to address what resources his thinking had and did not have. While the critique of political economy is, descriptively, incredibly germane and interesting – in particular Marx's remarks on credit in volume three of *Capital*: it's tremendously prescient – the issue of the political agent and the political subject in

Marx has always been for me an open question. That began under the influence of someone like Ernesto Laclau, who was trying to accept a Marxian analysis of the state of the world but then to rethink the nature of political subjectivity and collective-will formation in Marx by using Gramsci. Gramsci has always been a huge influence on me. He always seemed to be the most intelligent and reasonable Marxist.

SJ: You are still working with the concept of hegemony in *Infinitely Demanding*.

SC: Yes, I just think that politics is about hegemony. It's about the formation of a collective will or a common sense, the formation of what Laclau would call a chain of equivalences. You can link up different interest groups with very different conceptions of the good around a common struggle. That's a kind of value-neutral remark. It's as true, in fact it's truer, on the right as on the left. Until the rise of Obama in the US, it was the right that was using that technique in politics particularly well. Hegemony is just the logic of politics for me.

The drift towards anarchism has just been an increasing frustration with certain forms of Marxism. It seems to me that the political sequence that emerges into media visibility with the Seattle protests in November 1999 is best captured with an idea of anarchism. So it's a question of trying, with activist groups and friends and different people, to rethink the nature of anarchism. This has led me towards the position you find in *Infinitely Demanding* – a book that is very much a first statement.

I've always been very persuaded by Bakunin's critique of Marx. In the sense that Marxists are crypto-Bismarckian: they're secret lovers of the state form and they crave new forms of authority. The anarchist tradition is one that has always been peripheral to that. Its big impact has been in

Slavic and Latin countries. The great anarchist thinkers are Russian and Italian. Academically, it's interesting that Marxism has always been such a success in the academy. It works incredibly well because you've got an elaborate theory that you can discuss the nature of: Marxist theory and its relationships to developments. There's a series of very difficult books to read so it works well in seminars.

SJ: It offers a model of analysis that can be applied endlessly and discussed in these applications with considerable nuance.

SC: Yes, and it's very amenable to theorization, whereas anarchism has always been suspicious of that. That goes back to the Bakunin–Marx relation. Bakunin never really gets it together. His writings are interventions: letters and occasional texts. Nothing adds up to the sort of theoretical edifice that Marx produced. There is a reluctance among many anarchist groups to theorize their activity or practice. For them, the practice is the thing and the theorization is to miss it. I think that's why there are fewer anarchists in the academy. It's a contextual discourse in the sense that it is a theory of politics based on mutual aid, cooperation, the idea of direct democracy, and the rest. It is inherently much more plausible, say, in this context I'm working in now than in forms of academified Marxism. There's a certain self-consciousness within American political and religious discourse around ideas of small-scale communities, usually religious communities, which are implicitly anarchist. It works. It seems more plausible here. It's also closer to the way in which activist groups actually function: in terms of a disparate range of groups with often very different interests, often connected with single issues, or often connected with religious commitments. So the heart of anarchism for me is not a set of theoretical commitments, as with Marxism, but a set of ethical concerns with practice.

SJ: I'm interested in discussing your relation to the wider anarchist tradition. Could you consider yourself a kind of mutualist because the ethical demand you are concerned with in *Infinitely Demanding* draws us away from individualism towards a more mutual experience of society?

SC: Yes. I'm happy to be described as a mutualist, though the recent work that I've been doing is on mystical anarchism. This material is a strange new departure for me but my implicit prejudice or assumption is that human beings are not inherently wicked. Human beings in the right circumstances – and they are not in the right circumstances – are capable of behaving cooperatively and on the basis of trust if they are allowed to. It's the state's law, bureaucracy, and the rest which hinders that. I see human wickedness as a sociohistorical outcome rather than a natural fact. This is what takes me back to the importance of original sin and the relationship between original sin and politics. It seems to me that all forms of authoritarianism rely on some idea of original sin. If you believe in some idea of essential human defectiveness, then you are going to be led towards some form of authoritarianism as a way of rectifying that defectiveness – through the institutions of the church and the state and all the rest.

So I'm implicitly a mutualist. The question is: what's possible at the present moment? I've got different views on that. I think we're stuck with the state form, more or less; it's a pity that we're stuck with it but I think that we are stuck with it for the foreseeable future. Anarchism is about federalism. It's about a federalistic politics. There are times when I could imagine the European Union going over to a radical form of federalism if it decided to abandon its commitment to the nation-state. You could imagine a radically decentralized European area based on a federation of cities, villages, and all the rest where the economy would be returned to localities in a very dramatic way.

SJ: Irish politics, for instance, has traditionally defined itself in relation to the question of land and nationalism because of the colonial history with England. Perhaps with the rising influence of the European Union, with the euro, and the constant treaties, questions of nationalism will come to be less relevant. But surely there is a serious problem with the constitutionalism of the European Union.

SC: Sure, but what I'm saying is that to get from here to something better – that would be one way to move. You could imagine a genuine commitment to the overcoming of the nation-state which was the founding principle of the European Union. All the problems of constitutionalism, absolutely; but if people took that seriously, then you could imagine a much more developed form of federalism. The nation is a thing that appears at a certain point in European history, in moments of national romanticism, which arise as an anticolonial moment: Ireland, Finland. There's a book by Declan Kiberd on *Inventing Ireland*. Ireland is a very good example of the invention of a national myth. The nation was important at a certain point in political history but I would be interested in bringing about an end to that. That would be one way, a sort of real-world actual politics way, of thinking about forms of federalism that we could actually get to from where we are, even though there would be lots of problems with that. The anarchist tradition has always been this slightly impoverished, invisible, sort of underbelly to political thinking, which is always feeling misrepresented. It's a great pity.

SJ: To return a little towards Derrida and the question of theorizing what it means to be human: I accept that if we are to consider individuals to be bad, then this implies an authoritarian social politics – and Thomas Hobbes is a case in point. But if, on the other hand, you can be a little bit more optimistic about what it is to be a person alive today, then you can find yourself much more sympathetic to anarchist politics. Do you take seriously this question of the nature of humanity or would you still be working within a Derridean framework that would be suspicious of such essentialist questions?

SC: I take seriously the anthropological question. I don't think you can simply separate questions of politics from questions of humanity or, indeed, the nature of religion. These things are part and parcel. I also think that there is obviously an implicit humanistic prejudice in the way in which that question is posed – it's about the question of the human, the nature of the human, and we're still stuck with a humanistic metaphysics. One of the things that Derrida's work has persistently pointed out, or attempted to question, is that limit or frontier between the human and the animal or the human and the divine – and I take that seriously. In as much as Derrida is problematizing the question of the essence of the human, he is still asking that question, "What are 'The Ends of Man'"? It is not simply an issue of setting to one side all issues of human nature. It's a question of rethinking those categories in an essential way. That's one of the things that I take from Derrida's work. You can't simply say, "well, it's all discursively articulated and questions of nature needn't be considered." This is one sort of academic doxa you find. Another is, "well, it's all nature and it's all genetically coded in some way." These are obviously wrong. It seems that anarchism has had the capaciousness for thinking about forms of mutuality and cooperation that would question the limits of the human; and this goes back to deep spiritual traditions like the Franciscans and people like that. I think anarchism has always been out to question the idea of the human as the be-all and end-all of human existence.

SJ: You've already said that you can be considered sympathetic to mutualism and your discussion of cooperative federalism suggests a sympathy towards anarcha-syndicalism to a certain extent as well. Do you consider trade unions to be important?

SC: Trade unions are great for the most part. I used to be a union organizer in the 1980s in England, when I was still working there. I think that unions were absolutely essential at the time. I was also a Labour Party activist for many years in the 1980s and early 1990s. I left before Blair became leader. It still seems to me that unions are hugely important.

SJ: Perhaps the question is whether you consider trade unions a viable possibility for achieving social change. In *Infinitely Demanding*, you talk of political action in the interstices of the state. Would trade union activity be something that you have in mind or would you be thinking more about the summit protests? Where are these interstices?

SC: The interstices have to be created. I would begin from the idea that, at the present moment in history, the state saturates more and more areas of society. We live in societies of surveillance and control to an extent that would have been unimaginable a hundred years ago. It truly is a dystopian vision. To that extent, there is no space in the state. That's how the state works: it is by saturating the visibility of what takes place in the social terrain, and controlling it. The political system, the political machine, is what gives the impression of change within that state form. Forms of genuine resistance have to go about creating new spaces of visibility. I take the idea of "interstice" from Epicurus who says that the gods live in the interstices of space. There was an idea of God, a strange idea of God, that God was almost nonexistent but existing in the interstices and these interstices are ones which had to be articulated and created. They don't exist; they're not pre-given.

The example I give in *Infinitely Demanding* about indigenous rights protests works very well. There was no space for indigenous rights in Mexico in the 1980s. The space for indigenous rights had to be articulated through a struggle. This occurred in the context of a right that protected indigenous peoples, which the Mexican government had unwittingly granted when they signed a certain labor convention. It's around that that the movement took form and emerged into visibility. What happened with Seattle and after that was the emergence into visibility of a new form of resistance. That then becomes the interstice or a series of interstices. These are not pre-given; they have to be articulated. It becomes a question of how these interstices find a hook onto which they can attach themselves to the existing political system. It's a politics of protest.

SJ: It's interesting to hear that you derive the term interstice from Epicurus because I assumed it was from Hakim Bey's account of *Temporary Autonomous Zones*.

SC: That's something that I re-read about five or six years ago. It's on my mind as well. We tried to make a temporary autonomous zone at the New School in December 2009 with some of the students; we had an occupation which we declared to be a temporary autonomous zone. It was interesting. It was all about a fight over visibility. We had cameras in there and they were threatening to send the police in and whatever – it would have been bad publicity for the school – but there you go. Politics is about the creation of these spaces. What you do with these spaces then becomes . . . there are different options. One tradition would be secession, where you move away from the state as far as possible and set up your zone in the countryside or whatever. Another tradition would be to form that group into an organized political force that could exert pressure on the political system and the state, the way the Greens did in the 1970s, 1980s, and 1990s – say, in Germany, where they became part of the government in 1998, or around that time. There are different strategies you can adopt at that point. For me, there is a question mark over the nature of resistance and protest. I think that the political sequence that emerges into political visibility with Seattle through to the G7 protests has come to an end or is coming to an end. Strategically, tactically, there was the element of surprise in Seattle. People didn't know how to deal with these new tactics and now they do. What one does next – I think I mentioned this in Dublin recently – I was talking about an activist group in France, the Invisible Committee . . .

SJ: Yes, you mentioned them. *The Call* is the name of their text, isn't it?

SC: Yes, Yes. They've got this idea of zones of opacity. In many ways, this is just the question for me – that the Seattle sequence was all about the emergence into more and more powerful forms of visibility. The use of spectacular, huge protests to make a political point. Maybe different tactics are necessary at this point. I don't really know what to suggest but I'm talking to people, and listening to people, and reading things, and I'm just curious.

SJ: Isn't the spectacle to which you have just referred a threatening kind of logic? To conceive of political action within this spectacular sphere risks creating news reports but no change. The problem I'm gesturing towards is the problem of direct action and whether direct action is actually possible. Or are we trapped within the symbolic creation of identity and of news rather than political change?

SC: I think that there is an absolute risk of that. One risks replicating the spectacle in and through forms of resistance and successful resistance is resistance that gets the right publicity, that creates the right effect. A few students of mine unfurled a "free Tibet" banner outside one of the Olympic areas in Beijing last year. It took months of coordinated action and they had to build the thing there and it was only up for 30 seconds before the police tore it down and they were all arrested. But they got a picture in the *New York Times* and elsewhere. Now that's effective protest at a certain level but at another level it's just the creation of news. I think that this is always a difficult thing to think about. The politics of resistance shouldn't exhaust itself by trying to appeal to a news agenda. There's no question about that, but it can't afford to ignore it. It's a really tricky one. What interests me a lot more is the fact that you get a bunch of people in a room who have thought carefully about these issues and you can come to interesting forms of consensus and thoughtfulness about what should be done. I think that direct action is essential but over the means of direct action there is a question mark for me. A certain sequence has come to an end, I think. It's a question mark as to what is going to happen in the immediate future. The issue is what happens on the ground. It's about people organizing quasi-institutions for themselves that they have autonomy over, whether that's a food co-op or some sort of medical cooperative or some kind of free school or whatever it might be. Those are the important things. While I think that it's something that has been much more a part of the anarchist movement, I feel that it is something that has often remained below the level of visibility. Its great successes have often been less than visible. Anarchism has been making waves in political history over the last 170 years – well, longer than that if you go back to Godwin – and it's had a huge number of small successes that it doesn't really celebrate as much as it perhaps should. The image of anarchism as violent, crazy protest, which goes back to the end of the nineteenth century, is still one that people very much struggle with. That disappoints me. Changing the image of anarchism would be one thing that could be done – go on CNN and say that anarchists are nice people.

SJ: It can be difficult to create these freer spaces of activity in society and maybe this is something about the difficulty of the state.

SC: Yes, I think so.

SJ: One of the key aspects of the Levinasian understanding of anarchy is the overcoming of individual autonomy. Does it make sense to theoretically conceptualize the end of individual autonomy – which is quite convincing on a number of levels – in the context of a political situation in which surveillance is often individual surveillance, where you are individualized by the forces, and operations of the state? Does this individualization simply become part of what is rejected?

SC: It's a good question. The point I'm trying to make in *Infinitely Demanding,* and in the work I've done around that topic subsequently, is to try to replace an idea of anarchism based on the idea of freedom, a humanist idea of individual freedom, with an anarchism of responsibility. To show, for instance, the anarchic form of organization in protests – like the antiwar protests or the antiglobalization protests – as based around the identification of a wrong rather than a claim for emancipation. A grievance in relation to a wrong. It's to try to show that the core of anarchism is not so much an idea of freedom but an idea of responsibility. If you read people like David Graeber, who is a friend of mine and brilliant on the issue of direct action, he has got an incredibly simple-minded idea of freedom and autonomy. The Levinasian dimension is that what anarchism is about is an experience of responsibility, infinite responsibility. What my argument against autonomy, a certain model of autonomy, is about is an idea of conscience. The *dividual*, in my parlance, is a way of thinking about the way that conscience structures and breaks apart what it means to be an individual. So in many ways – and this is a point that maybe could be made in relation to Derrida and Levinas – I'm not giving up individual autonomy. I'm trying to sort of radicalize it, deepen it, through an experience of heteronomy being called into question. If you like, the Levinasian and Derridean subject is more responsible than its individualistic, autonomous predecessor and autonomy is not a question of giving up. It becomes, as it were, exacerbated, radicalized, in a way. There are elements in thinkers like Levinas that could be very useful to anarchist groups.

SJ: You say that this ethical experience of the infinite demand is about an infinite responsibility requiring infinite commitment and an experience of conscience. Would you be able to expand on the experience of conscience in relation to this idea of the infinite demand? Is the infinite demand to act against something that is wrong, against injustice in society, or could it include acting in a way that isn't terribly ethical? In order to have responsibility for your actions, you have to bear the weight of them regardless of whether they are ethical or unethical?

SC: What do you mean by that? Well, yes, absolutely, you have to take responsibility both ways. The infinite demand, the way that the argument is structured, is that there is a motivational deficit in contemporary liberal democracy and this deficit is something that has to be supplemented at the level of subjectivity. The ethical demand is something that arises in relation to the particular other person who I am faced with. The demand that they exert on me is a demand that I could never meet. That's the basic intuition. *Not being able to meet that claim* is the condition not for paralysis but action in the world.

SJ: Is the ethical demand meta-ethical, what makes ethics in general possible, or does it have a normative content?

SC: Both. The claim I make is that, meta-ethically, every conception of ethics has to derive from an idea of ethical experience and ethical subjectivity. Otherwise, it's empty and doesn't address itself to the subject for whom it is intended; it becomes some kind of mechanism or procedure and fails to address the problem of motivation – the moral psychological question. Meta-ethically, all conceptions of morality have to be linked back to the idea of ethical demand and the approval of that demand.

SJ: Ethical opinions and judgments inform struggles for hegemony over the ethical sphere in society. For example, if you come to an issue like abortion from a certain anarchist perspective, then it is a question of whether the state is entitled to exercise its authority over a woman's body. What happens when you approach an issue such as abortion from the point of view of the ethical demand? Does the ethical demand suggest a different position on abortion?

SC: No, it doesn't. That would be a political question for me. The way in which this works is that the level of ethics is about picking out a structure of ethical subjectivity and trying to show how that works. To fill that with specific judgments or views is more of a political task for me. Perversely, I can imagine both a pro-lifer and a pro-choicer having an overwhelming sense of a demand. There are billboards with anti-abortion adverts all over this part of Florida with "Life begins at conception" and "If you're pregnant, you have a choice." Now that's a certain ethical demand based on a certain set of metaphysical presumptions about the nature of life and its relation to the divine. The infinite ethical demand at its most abstract level is neutral with regard to that. It's a question of building-in particular judgments.

SJ: Let's take into account the particular forms that the ethical demand can take in society, or the forms that the ethical demands have taken historically. An example would be the demand to be a good housewife and obey patriarchal institutions. That is clearly a demand for hierarchy, a social pressure placed on people in the form of an "ethical" demand. In *Infinitely Demanding*, you claim that there is something intrinsically democratizing about the ethical demand, or that it necessarily leads to a radical politics.

SC: Not necessarily. The claim I make is that democratization is action, based on an ethical demand. There's no necessity to that; it's a question of construction at that point. Nothing flows deductively from the fact of the ethical demand right the way down to real world politics.

SJ: That's both good and bad.

SC: Yes, this is the error of a Habermasian position: that if you can get the right transcendental picture, you can go all the way from that to democratic deliberation. The ethical demand is something that can be repressive and has been repressive. My meta-ethical claim is that all conceptions of morality flow from an idea of the ethical demand. That demand has for the most part been a repressive demand. There is no question about that, but it's not a question of being liberated from that, but an issue of how one can think about restructuring that demand and make it one's own.

Then it becomes a question of linking that constructively to forms of political action. There's no deduction there from one thing to another. It's a constructive task, if you like. You could say that there is something democratizing about the ethical demand insofar as it's a commitment to equality. You could say that, but how it would actually work in practice would be a political issue.

SJ: Yes, because there is a tension between the general philosophical notion of equality and the specific question of what that would actually mean in a given social situation.

SC: Sure, and the strength of the anarchist tradition for me has always been its commitment to locality. Politics is not a top-down business and that, for me, is the problem with Marxism. It's always the other way around. It's a question of looking at forms of local activity, local processes, and local defeats and victories. These become sites for the emergence of a demand that has a much more general function than that, instead of the other way around. What interests me in the history of anarchism is that you can go back to the Diggers in the English revolution. The action they take is the possession of the land and they engage in planting vegetables and trying to cultivate the land. That's an actual practice that develops and at the heart of that is a demand that is being articulated. They say that things will not go right in England until goods are held in common. I take the point very seriously. Particularly when you're reading a philosophical text on ethics and politics, it can look as if it's the other way around. I'm not interested in that. I'm interested in – and this is a phenomenological commitment – actual forms of life, and existence, and pulling out structures from them.

SJ: A question about terminology. You use the term "demand" and it suggests a way of getting motivation back into the description of how ethics actually works because the demand draws the individual out of themselves and into social and political action on an ethical basis. Why is it a demand at all and what is the authority that makes this demand possible as a demand? It suggests that the individual makes no gift of themselves to ethics.

SC: There is no demand without the approval of the demand. If a demand does not have approval, then it is coercion. So it's a delicate operation and there are forms of demand which are . . . think of it in terms of Christianity. Most people who are Christians believe that there is an ethical demand which the fact of Christ conveys upon human beings.

SJ: That they are convinced by the Bible.

SC: Yes, there are people for whom the demand flows from the commandments of God – there's a higher authority to that demand; the demand is exercised upon the Christian by the fact of Christ's death and resurrection. People would say that that demand flows from a command, which is the whole theology of Christianity. Then there are people who would say, like Alasdair MacIntyre, that the command doesn't matter. And I'm very sympathetic to MacIntyre on this point. The essential element of Christianity is the fact that there is a demand that one imposes on oneself. Whether that demand flows from the fact that there was this God–man on a mission or not is neither here nor there. Then you get very close to the idea that the demand is the demand for the person who approves of that demand and freely accepts it. The coercion that is exerted is a kind of self-coercion. I put myself under a demand, freely, and that's what conscience would be in that sense.

SJ: It still seems to me that this notion of motivation linked to a demand is operating within a structure of thought that sets up the ability to approve of something, as a kind of individual action, against a demand for someone to act that is necessarily authoritarian. It does not seem very far away from the conceptual structure at work in the legal system, where you have a conception of individuals acting freely, while simultaneously subject to imposed legal demands. You seem to be operating with some kind of autonomy and some kind of authority in a problematic way in your conception of the *dividual*. Problematic in this sense: you are interested in going beyond the orthodoxy of the autonomy of the individual while, at the same time, you are interested in anarchism – with the implied move away from authoritarian ways of being-together as people.

SC: The demand is self-authorizing. The demand without an approval is sheer coercion. Autonomy would be the thought that the approval and the demand are equal to each other. Classically, in Kant's moral philosophy, freedom and the moral law are mirrors of each other. All legitimate conceptions of morality have to be self-authorizing. I begin from that, but the authority that the ethical demand lays upon me is not something that I'm equal to. If I were equal to it, then that would be a classical form of autonomy. The Levinasian thought is that I put myself under a demand that I could never meet. So rather than being a way of contradicting autonomy, it's a way of deepening autonomy – of showing its hetero-affective constitution of self-authorization. This is very close to Derrida; it's an exacerbation of the experience of responsibility or unconditional hospitality.

5 Action in a World of Recuperation

Cynicism and the Slovenian Hamlet

Carl Cederström

BLACK'S CLUB, LONDON, JUNE 2008

In 2008, Critchley and Slavoj Žižek had crossed swords in the London Review of Books *and* Harper's Magazine *in an ongoing disagreement over the status of political violence. Žižek had accused Critchley of promoting an untenable distance from the state, as a form of political resistance. Critchley fired back: Žižek's rhetoric of violence was in fact an aversion to concrete political action. All of the talk about revolutionary acts of violence was just that (hence the epithet, the Slovenian Hamlet). This interview takes place in the wake of that exchange.*

Another important theme that arises is the political status of humor. Humor, Critchley has argued, is a potential site for political resistance. Yet politicians and corporations also employ this tactic for their own motives. What are we to make of the appropriation of humor by institutions of power? A further topic is that of the relationship between mysticism and psychosis. While some of the ideas that were developed here came to be included in a chapter on mystical anarchism in Critchley's forthcoming book, The Faith of the Faithless, *others "went nowhere and will go nowhere."*

The interview took place in London, at Black's Club in the heart of Soho. "Black's Club was a haunt of mine, a favorite spot. Whenever I go back to London I always go there. It's a lovely Bohemian place."

Action in a World of Recuperation

CARL CEDERSTRÖM: You have said that a common response to today's politics is a passive withdrawal from the world. Let's begin with how you would like to define, or diagnose, the present political situation.

SIMON CRITCHLEY: I have at least three political categories for thinking of the present situation: military neoliberalism, neo-Leninism, and neo-anarchism. Among these three, I think that military neoliberalism is what best characterizes the state of the western world. At the heart of this category is the idea of a unification of neoliberal economics with a certain universalization of democracy and human rights talk – which is ultimately backed up with military force. So the situation we're in is one where other regimes have to accept the logic of capitalism, accept the ideology of democracy and human rights – and if they don't accept that, they're going to be bombed. That's the logic of military neoliberalism. The world is in a state of permanent war, in a state of chaos. In the face of a world that is blowing itself to pieces, where, as Dostoyevsky says, "blood is being spilt in the merriest ways, as if it were champagne," it is tempting to withdraw, make yourself into an island, close your eyes and pretend nothing bad goes on. This response – which is both plausible and coherent, but which I like to refuse – is what I call passive nihilism.

CC: But the opposite response – to actively engage in politics, to dutifully go to the voting booth, to publicly express your opinions – couldn't that also be a way of distancing yourself? At least this is what Žižek seems to claim in his book *On Violence*: that sometimes "doing nothing is the most violent thing you could do."

SC: I'm simply not in agreement with Žižek here. His argument is that in a world defined by systemic violence –

actual violence, as well as symbolic violence – one needs to step back, reflect, and wait. For me, this is the obsessional neurotic position – and that's why I have called Žižek, in the response I wrote for *Harper's Magazine*, the "Slovenian Hamlet." Hamlet lives in a world defined by violence, where time is out of joint, where one's father is killed illegitimately, and where the order of kings and social hierarchies has broken down, and as a result Hamlet cannot act; he dreams of an act of vengeance, for which he lacks the courage, and ends up doing nothing. In Žižek, you also find this horror of the immediacy of action. He will say things like, "I have a hat but I don't have a rabbit." I think that's overly pessimistic, although I can understand the diagnosis. What interests me are forms of resistance that take into account the situation we're in, but which don't stop there – forms of resistance that go on and try to act in new imaginative ways. This is where neo-anarchism comes in: as the articulation of the possibility of new forms of coalition, new chains of equivalence; and in that regard, unlike Žižek, I'm not dismissive of anti-capitalist movements of resistance and protest.

CC: This leads us to what seems to be Žižek's main critique against your work: that the forms of resistance you advocate, forms of resistance that retain a distance from the state, are futile.

SC: Yes. The argument that Žižek makes against me is that these demands are powerless – that they don't change anything. He's right and he's wrong. In a way, all forms of resistance are powerless. You could even say that the history of political resistance is one long history of failure. The student protest in Paris, 1968, was a failure: the events took place in May, and already on June 23, 1968, De Gaulle was elected back into power. And the list of failures goes on. What we should remember is that the effects of resistance are often experienced retrospectively. I think that to judge political resistance by the standards of its effectiveness at the level of political power within the terrain of the state is a delusion – a Leninist delusion. The argument here is really an argument of state power versus no power. For Žižek, resistance is futile; resistance is surrender. We have to occupy the terrain of the state, which is also the argument that Lenin makes in *The State and Revolution*. This is Lenin's critique of the anarchists: that the anarchists are unrealistic and bourgeois; that they lack the courage and ruthlessness to accept the cruelty of political reality. So what has to be done, according to Lenin, is an occupation of the state such that it eventually withers away. The obvious historical objection is that this never happened. Instead, the Bolshevik revolution led to the most grotesque elevation of the state, in the form of the Soviet Union, and to human disasters. So it could be said that the debate between Žižek and myself is really a debate between Lenin and anarchism, or between Marx and Bakunin. Bakunin, in his critique in the 1870s, calls Marx a crypto-Bismarckian. He says that what Marxists secretly want, at all costs, is state power. I, contrary to Lenin and Žižek, argue for politics as the hegemonic articulation of an interstitial distance from state power that cannot simply be judged by the standard of whether power has been taken or not. And with regard to the other issue – whether capitalism is here to stay or not – I think Žižek accepts that. I also accept it, but in a much more melancholic spirit. Who knows, with the current global economic crisis, perhaps a certain model of capitalism is coming to an end. Perhaps we are living through the beginning of the end.

CC: An important addition to this formula is comedy, more precisely, how humor opens up new avenues for resistance.

How does your notion of the comic subject of politics differ from the classical subject of politics?

SC: The classical subject of politics is a virile, active, autarchic, sovereign subject – a subject that *can* – a subject that is able to act. For me, that goes together with a certain lack of humor, whether that is Bush or bin Laden. They are both active, virile political subjects, engaged in some sort of bloody contest. What interests me about comedy as a form of resistance is that comedy is the performance of powerlessness. The comic subject doesn't assume that it has power; it doesn't assume its virility. It performs its powerlessness in acts of nonviolent warfare – it is the power of the powerless. So classical political subjects are capable of acting; they are virile, they are potent, and they are humorless. But most importantly they are "justified" in what they do. What interests me is to think of a political subjectivity that would find itself inescapably involved in acts which cannot be justified. I've been doing some work recently on Benjamin's critique of violence and there's a fascinating argument in Benjamin where he says that "law is violence, politics is violence, but does violence exhaust the political field?" And his answer is no. There's a guideline of nonviolence, which to him is expressed in the biblical prohibition of murder: "Thou shall not kill." The situation in which that prohibition arises is a situation of violence: I know I cannot kill and yet I'm in a situation where I have to kill. The violence that I perpetrate is necessary but not justified. To think about an idea of politics based upon a non-justifiable sphere of violence is fascinating. This is similar to Judith Butler's claim about mourning. The classical political subject doesn't want to mourn, but to act. After 9/11, there were 11 days of mourning. Then mourning was declared to be over and it was time for action. The question that Judith Butler asks, which I find enormously interesting, is what a politics of grief and mourning would look like – a politics based around the powerlessness of grief and mourning.

CC: At the same time, it has become increasingly popular among politicians to either mock themselves, or happily subject themselves to mockery. Take Stephen Colbert's talk at the White House Correspondents' Dinner, for example, where he scornfully delivered jokes at Bush's expense. Would this be an example of a powerful critique directed against the Bush administration or, on the contrary, a type of humor which is easily co-opted and turned into something positive for the Bush campaign?

SC: I think Stephen Colbert's mocking of Bush was a classic example of political satire, and a very powerful satire. It was nicely painful. I thought to myself, when I saw it, that this is a courageous act, this is a powerful thing. But sure, it could be co-opted. Political leaders can use humor in all sorts of ways. We should always remember that humor is radically situational and contextual. It can always be redescribed in toothless ways.

CC: Let us stay with the relation between humor and co-optation a little longer. In the world of business organizations there seems to be an obsession with having fun, being happy, or acting a bit on the crazy side. We see this in many organizations, of which Google is probably the most conspicuous example. Employees, it seems, become obliged to participate in silly activities or whatever the organization finds humorous. Does this preempt the possibility of powerfully using humor as a form of resistance?

SC: I actually gave a talk at Google recently, part of their authors@google program. They wanted me to speak about humor, so I went there and dutifully gave my views on humor. Of course, that's a classic strategy of co-optation. But I gave an example there, which is from my book *On Humour*, concerning the way in which corporations deal with humor. The example is from a hotel in Atlanta, where I was staying. When having breakfast one morning, I saw a group of employees in one of these huge rooms, this sort of windowless suite you'll find in American hotels. They were engaging in structured fun: playing kick-ball, ping-pong, Frisbee, whatever – you know – these forms of fun and humor that are being used in order to build up the morale amongst employees. In this way, humor becomes a form of compulsory happiness – it becomes a strategy that organizations use to impose a compulsory happiness. If you don't go along with the structured fun, you're no fun, you're a party-pooper. In that sense, humor can be used by organizations as a form of coercion. When I was in the Google office, I saw people running around on scooters. They've also got a vast recreation room with ping-pong and plastic balls where you could exercise and have fun with your colleagues. This means that the line between work and play becomes increasingly difficult to draw, which by extension means that work never ceases – that even play becomes another form of work; structured fun becomes a way in which the corporation regulates and organizes the behavior of its employees. To that extent, I think humor is extremely dangerous.

To go back to the example in Atlanta: after having watched the people engaging in structured fun, I met a number of them outside, smoking cigarettes and talking to each other. I asked if they were really free to refuse to take part in this or not. And they said that they were free to refuse, but they would have been seen as bad employees or party- poopers. So they weren't really given a choice as to whether they wanted to be involved or not. But while smoking, they started to engage in a series of small jokes, talking about what a shit the manager who was organizing this was, and so on and so forth. So by standing there, smoking and telling obscene jokes, they created a nonorganizational exterior space, where they could be themselves.

So humor works in two ways in organizations. On the one hand, it can be a coercive mechanism for producing false harmony amongst the workforce. But on the other hand, the informal circulation of humor, which occurs particularly through dirty, obscene humor, can never be controlled. When I was working in factories in the late 1970s, that's the way humor worked: really disgusting jokes, such as photocopied sheets of paper with vast sexual organs penetrating the secretary of the boss or the boss himself. So humor is about regulation but can still, informally, have a subversive potential. What we have seen, though, in the last 20 to 30 years is the use of humor consultants, so-called fun-sultants, which study organizations in order to improve their spirit or ethos. And this I find oppressive.

CC: But could we think of something like an ethical corporation, where the use of, say, humor could have a subversive effect?

SC: Can corporations be ethical? I'm not sure. I would say that if they can, it is with great difficulty. Corporations, by definition, incorporate. The corporation is a sort of vast body, which you have to be part of. From a political perspective, the corporation is a totalitarian structure by necessity. Moments of ethics would occur in those moments of obscene informal contact, when people say what they really think. But the flipside of subversion is recuperation. This lesson comes from the Situationists. Strategies of subversion, or what the Situationists call *détournement*, are always recuperable. And again, subversion in humor is radically context-specific. Certain jokes, at certain times, will subvert the situation. But that same joke can be employed by the organization, and turned into something positive, even an appetizer. When people complained that Stella Artois beer was too expensive, they internalized the criticism and turned it into their selling point, reassuring in their slogan that their beer was expensive. This is a common strategy by which a critique becomes recuperated as an organizational appetizer slogan. It's always like that. The limit of subversion, or the place at which subversion can take place, is constantly moving. New forms of humor are powerful only for a brief period of time, after which they can be deployed by the very forces they were originally set out to laugh at. I think this is true of every form of humor. What that means is not that humor is useless, but that in any organizational framework there will be new forms of informal subversive wit, usually centered around obscenity. Obscenity is interesting because there might be a limit to the obscene that might not be recuperable. The obscene is an interesting category.

CC: It is an interesting category indeed, and one that has been explored by a number of psychoanalysts over the years, perhaps most extensively by Lacan – which leads me to the next question. Your relation to Lacanian psychoanalysis seems ambiguous, if not critical. For instance, in *Infinitely Demanding*, you criticize Lacan and Lacanians for having distorted the picture of human finitude by making the subject too heroic, too authentic.

SC: Yes, my relation to Lacan is ambiguous. In *Infinitely Demanding* and *Ethics, Politics, Subjectivity*, I claim that Lacan is heir to a tragic heroic paradigm that begins with German idealism. My main disagreement with Lacan, and the tragic paradigm as a whole, concerns a supposed link between heroism and authenticity. This comes out of my critique of Heidegger, in particular. What Heidegger is up to in *Being and Time* – at least this is my understanding – is that you must choose your hero: either you choose *das Man*, the inauthentic life, or you choose yourself – the point being that you have to choose yourself as your hero in order to be authentic. My main critique of Lacan boils down to a critique of linking authenticity with heroism, and I believe that argument has some plausibility. Badiou, however, has an interesting response to this argument. He says that we could speak of a heroism of the void: a heroism which is not a heroism of authenticity, but a heroism of the divided subject. This means that heroism, rather than being the completion of the subject in authenticity, becomes the name of the evisceration of the subject in the face of an uncontrollable Event.

CC: Badiou's reading mainly concerns *Seminar VII*, but in the late Lacan the heroic subject is no longer based on an idea of pure desire.

SC: There are of course other aspects of Lacan – there are other Lacans, as it were – and in this regard I am happy to accept that my critique has its limitations. When I'm being defensive, I say that I'm just talking about *Seminar VII*, which is also what Žižek calls the heroic moment in Lacan's teaching, appearing in the late 1950s. In Lacan's later work, it is clear that something else happens. In *Ethics, Politics, Subjectivity*, I say that there is this tragic heroic moment, but that there is also a moment of comedy. Lacan's genius in that seminar is to focus on the mute figure of Harpo Marx as an image of *das Ding*. The play of jokes and the comedy of the Marx brothers, I would say, is also an articulation of the relation to the ethical subject and the real.

I'm thinking now of doing some work on psychosis. The idea is that there seems to be a relation between psychosis and mysticism. The mystic tries to empty itself, annihilate itself, in order to be filled with divine love. So the mystic achieves that glorification of subjectivity through touching the divine. The material body is important here because it is through the wounding, or the marking, of the body that the psychotic tries to communicate, and become unified, with God. We find exactly the same structure in the psychosis of Schreber, or, indeed, in the psychotics whom I've come across. The material body becomes a body that is only completed in relation to the divine. In a sense, the psychotic cannot complete their own body image without it.

CC: Are there any particular philosophers who would symbolize this form of mystical psychosis?

SC: The philosopher who comes to mind as the classic psychotic would be Spinoza. In Spinoza, you have the idea that through the use of reason, you attain an intellectual understanding of the divine, of plenitude, of nature. This is what he calls "beatitude." The structure we find in both mysticism and psychosis – the unification of the glorified body with the divine – can also be found in certain philosophical systems, driven by that same fantasy of unifying the human with the divine. You could find that, as already mentioned, in Spinoza. You can find that in the hermetic tradition, with people like Giordano Bruno. You can also find that in Simone Weil, who was emptying out her body, physically, by self-starvation. She dies an anorexic death: starving herself to death, while at the same point reaching a communion with God, which is a form of divinization of the self.

CC: Speaking of death, there's a growing interest in transhumanist studies and other related fields where increased longevity and, ultimately, immortality are conceived not only as desirable, but possible. This usually comes with the idea of moving away from the human as we know it, to the post-human. What is your relation to this discourse?

SC: I think it is a terrible, pernicious, delusion. I think the idea that we become mind, that the human condition could be perfected through infinite longevity, is a recurrent delusion in the history of thought. I want to flip things around and say that what should be questioned in western culture is the idea of longevity – that a good life is the same thing as a long life, a long life underwritten by medical science and developments in technology. I claim that the material condition for the possibility of being human is the body. The body withers and dies, it lessens and changes, and that is the constant reminder of who we are. For me, to be *free* is to accept the limitation of one's body, accepting oneself as a material and mortal being. That involves accepting that life is brief, and that life has to be embraced, affirmed, and enjoyed in its brevity. I don't understand the idea of the post-human. I think the human is a sick animal, maybe even an evolutionary mistake. But that's where we are. So my work on the idea of disappointment is an acceptance of limitation: limitation, not merely as something limiting, but as the condition of possibility for flourishing, of freedom and life. Montaigne says that he who has learned how to die has unlearned how to be a slave. What he means is that he who has accepted the limit of mortality has become free. Therefore the idea of living for a thousand years is slavery for me. As simple as that. It is an ideology of human enslavement: a delusion which is bound up to an ideology of the future. For at least the last 500 years, there has been the fantasy that in the next 50 years there will be developments such that will enable us to live for ever. This future is a tiny bit further away than we can imagine, but not that far. I think it's dreadful. There will certainly be a future, but any sort of faith in the future is a superstition. I believe that the only way of facing the future is by turning towards the past and listening to the counsel of the dead, the hard lessons of history.

This interview was published previously as Critchley, "Philosophy in the Boudoir and the Streets: An Interview with Simon Critchley," *Ephemera* 9(1) (2009): 44–51.

6 Language and Murder

Blanchot, Stevens, and the Literary

Tom McCarthy, Penny McCarthy, Anthony Auerbach,
Victoria Scott, and Paul Perry for the International
Necronautical Society

Austrian Cultural Institute, London, March 2001

*This sixth interview was Critchley's first exchange with the artist
and novelist Tom McCarthy (who was recently short-listed for the
Booker Prize). "This was a fateful encounter," Critchley explains.
General Secretary McCarthy and his fellow members of the
International Necronautical Society (INS) – a semi-fictitious art col-
lective, exploring death – had turned the Austrian Cultural Forum
into an interrogation room, and Simon was one of the first in a series
of cultural figures who was hauled up in front of the committee.
About six months later, Simon was invited to become INS's Chief
Philosopher. "I thought that Tom was brilliant, and we became
really close friends very quickly. We began to write together, first on
Joyce, then on Shakespeare."*

*The interview covers a wide range of literary and philosophical
references, from Ponge and Stevens to Blanchot to Bataille. One of
the central topics raised is materiality and its relation to language.
Is language murder, as Blanchot says, or can we remain attentive
and receptive to the objects we set out to describe, such that they can
keep on "living," or persisting in their singularity and particularity?
Ponge and Stevens are of interest in this regard as each is sensitive to
language; they both avoid a corruption or annihilation of their objects
of interest. Apart from investigations into poetry, this discussion also
goes into the relation between humor and the Holocaust. While this*

might first appear an unlikely coupling, their suture arrives in the work of Beckett, the definitive literary hero for both Critchley and McCarthy.

TOM McCARTHY: You write in your book *Very Little . . . Almost Nothing* that the task of philosophical modernity is the thinking through of the first death, the *über*-death, which is the death of God. So my first question is what is the meaning of this death?

SIMON CRITCHLEY: It's a big question. Nietzsche said "God is dead," and that's written on toilet walls all over the world. But he then went on to say: "And we have killed him." So modernity, by which I mean that social, economic, and intellectual process that begins in the early seventeenth century, culminates in the fact that we no longer require God as a metaphysical underpinning for our beliefs. So the death of God is part of a historical process. And philosophy, at a certain point – it's arguable when that starts – also shifts its emphasis. In medieval philosophy, human beings were creatures, and all creatures were dependent on a creator who was himself uncreated, the self-caused cause of everything, a *causa sui*. So God was at the center of the web, holding the universe together. With the advent of the modern world, that focus moves to the human subject – so that for someone like Descartes, the first point of certainty in a philosophical system is no longer the existence of God but the existence of the self.

Now, the problem with that is that the nice thing about God and religion is that it provides an answer to the question of the meaning of life. It does this by positing something outside of earthly life, the divine order. So the death of God, in a sense, is unimportant; what's important is that it raises the question of the meaning of life. But what is the meaning of life if there can be no religious basis to the meaning of life? There are various responses to that. One obvious response is that if religion is no longer the realm in which the question of the meaning of life is to be thought through, then what other realm is? One obvious candidate is art. Art becomes the way that questions of the meaning and value of life are articulated; and the aesthetic movement associated with that is Romanticism. In Romanticism, the energy of religion gets transformed into an artwork: an artwork that would reveal God, or something like God, in nature – but what that actually means is that artworks provide meaning for a human self. For the German Romantics such as Schlegel, the aesthetic form capable of bearing that question of meaning is the novel, and the task becomes writing the great novel of the modern world. And then different spheres take up that same challenge over the next 200 years. If you're a Marxist, you believe that realm of meaning is fundamentally socio-economic, for example.

TMcC: There's something that confuses me, which perhaps confused Nietzsche as well. The madman who announces the death of God in that passage from *The Gay Science* paints a horrific picture of skies decomposing and the world getting darker and darker all the time. It's not a great joyous liberation; there's an absolute terror there. But then elsewhere in Nietzsche there is a sense of joy, albeit an ambiguous one: we must go forwards in joyous terror and terrible joy and so on. So is Nietzsche ultimately happy or sad that God is dead? Or is he just stating a fact?

SC: What makes Nietzsche interesting as a thinker is that he's full of a religious passion. Nietzsche's real twin intellectually is someone like St Paul. He's much closer to him than John Locke or David Hume. Nietzsche is traumatized by the death of God because he realizes that it's a collapse of the basis of meaning. You find a similar line of thought in Dostoyevsky. Dostoyevsky says that the only thing that keeps humans above the level of cattle is the belief in the immortality of the soul. The name for this problem is nihilism. In my work, I've tried to place the question of nihilism at the center of philosophical concerns. Nihilism is the situation where, as Nietzsche says, the highest values devalue themselves: *Daß die obersten Werte sich entwerten*. The death of God is part of that process: God has become empty, nothing. The philosopher who most represents that position for Nietzsche is Schopenhauer – and what he calls "European Buddhism." In fact, we could think about the whole contemporary interest in Buddhism as a way of thinking about the nihilism problem: Nothing has any meaning, therefore I'll affirm the void, and I'll engage in practices of the self – yoga, tantric sex . . .

TMcC: Is that where devaluation slips over into transvaluation?

SC: In one sense, yes: nothing has any value, so I'll affirm the nothing – nothing is the guarantor of meaning. But Nietzsche refuses that: that's just exoticism. So the task facing the philosopher, and also the artist, is one of responding to nihilism. What people always get wrong with Nietzsche is calling him a nihilist. Nietzsche is *diagnosing* nihilism in modern culture. It's that question, the question of nihilism, that I want to put at the center of my agenda. It's not a question that is central for much philosophy in the English-speaking world. It's a question that's been deemed to be almost indecent because in a sense we can ironize our way out of it.

VICTORIA SCOTT: Can you explain the difference between passive and active nihilism?

SC: Reading Nietzsche is like reading the Bible, in that it's a question of interpretation, and there are various ones. Nihilism as a theme is explored in *The Will to Power*, which is put together by his nasty fascist sister, so it's a miscellany, a collection of fragments. Books One and Two deal with nihilism, and early on in Book One there's a discussion of passive nihilism and active nihilism. My interpretation is that passive nihilism is the European Buddhism I outlined a moment ago. Another version of passive nihilism would be to say, "Nothing is of any value, but hey, so what, we can just get along without any of this anxious metaphysical stuff." That would be pragmatism, as typified by Richard Rorty's response: he just shrugs his shoulders and says, "Nihilism was something that preoccupied certain highly strung European intellectuals in the nineteenth century. But we've gone beyond that."

Then there's active nihilism. Some people identify Nietzsche's position with active nihilism. Now, they're not *wrong*, but I think what Nietzsche means by active nihilism is what would have been reported in the press of his time as Russian nihilism: terrorism. Nietzsche picks up the idea of nihilism from the Russian novelist Turgenev. In Turgenev's *Fathers and Sons*, there's a conflict between the nihilist Bazarov and those who defend the status quo. So nihilism for Nietzsche was about a conflict within Russian culture between a pro-Europe, liberal, reformist view of Russia, on the one hand, and on the other people who believed in the creative power of destruction – through acts of violent insurrection – to overthrow the stale liberal order. These people called themselves nihilists; and they had an implicit belief in science. So Bazarov in Turgenev's book is very into science . . .

TMcC: Just like the anarchists Kropotkin or Bakunin.

SC: Yes. So that's what Nietzsche means by active nihilism. Which was then part of the drama of Turgenev's fiction, and also Dostoyevsky's. And there's a whole story about how that version of active nihilism moves through to Chernyshevsky and Bakunin and Lenin. In many ways, Bolshevism could be seen as active nihilism, the violent overthrow of the established order. There's a link as well between a scientific, positivist conception of the world and insurrection. Now, Nietzsche doesn't endorse that position at all. Essentially, he's neither a passive nor an active nihilist. He comes up with a third option, which he calls eternal return or eternal recurrence. Again, what that means is debatable. I've got an interpretation – do you want me to go into it? Nietzsche's response to nihilism is the doctrine of eternal return. You could read that in a cosmological way, as a belief that the universe is cyclical and is going to recur. I think that's all window dressing, though; I don't think that's what Nietzsche means. For him, eternal return is much more of a moral doctrine.

There's a story told by the poet Heinrich Heine about Kant walking on the heath with his servant, just after writing the first *Critique*, the *Critique of Pure Reason*, in which he takes God away. He looks at his servant and suddenly he feels so sorry for him – because he's taken God away from him – that he writes a second critique just to give God back. The essential thesis of the *Critique of Pure Reason* is that traditional metaphysics – which deals with God, freedom, and immortality – is cognitively meaningless. We cannot know whether God exists, whether the soul is immortal, and so on. That's the first *Critique*. Then in the second *Critique* Kant says, "But we can still maintain the idea of God, or immortality of the soul, as a postulate, a postulate of practical reason." So, although I cannot *know* whether God exists, I can still act as *if* he did, and that can orientate my ethical activity.

Nietzsche ups the ante and takes it a stage further. He says, "Well, this is ridiculous." What would it be to fully *affirm* the fact that God doesn't exist? To fully affirm the complete meaninglessness of the universe? And to be able to do that again and again and again. If you're capable of that thought, of affirming that this universe is not for us, that we're just here by sheer chance, and you can do that again and again, then you're equal to the force of eternal return. It's a sort of moral test.

TMcC: There seems to be an aesthetics of transformation going on in Nietzsche's thought, beyond the question of recurrence. Transfiguration is a meme that he offers up again and again.

SC: Yes. It's an almost physical practice – to be able to physically withstand that vertigo of meaninglessness and then transfigure oneself in relationship to that. I've got my doubts about that, but that's what Nietzsche says.

TMcC: Now, the other giant of philosophical modernity is Hegel, and death in his work seems to me to be even more central than it is in Nietzsche. How would you characterize Hegel's view of the relationship between death and knowledge?

SC: Death for Hegel is a conceptual process. But that's deceptive, because everything's a conceptual process for Hegel. But Hegel's notion of death would be that to conceptualize something is to kill it. So if I name this orange that's on the table here in front of us "an orange," insofar as I name it, it becomes separate and I deaden it. So in that sense Adam in the Garden of Eden was a serial killer.

TMcC: That's Kojève's take on it too, isn't it?

SC: Yes. Language is murder. Language, as conceptuality, is the murder of things by making them approximate to us. Then it becomes a question of the following: If language is murder, if creation is murder, then what does one then do

aesthetically? Blanchot talks about the two slopes of literature. There's one slope where the human subject compre-
hends everything by murdering it – which Blanchot would
identify with the Marquis de Sade. He puts Hegel and Sade
together. So sadist literature and sadist art would be the art
that kills its objects by conceptualizing them. Pornography
would be another example. Pornography captures its objects
by killing them. I think that's true: it's not just an objectifica-
tion of people; it's a killing of them too.

TMcC: Within that Blanchotian schema, would pornography be the model for all cognition?

SC: Yes, but then for him the other slope of literature would
be a form of art that leaves things to themselves in some
way. So I would write a poem about the orange that lets the
orange be the orange that it is, and this would put the reader
in the position of letting the orange, orange. Letting things
thing.

TMcC: So someone like Francis Ponge . . .

PENNY MCCARTHY: Or Wallace Stevens . . .

SC: Stevens is the greatest philosophical poet of the twentieth century in the English language – full stop – in my
humble opinion. And Ponge, who writes these lovely poems
about oysters . . . And Rilke, Rilke's *Duino Elegies*. What do
you say to the angel? What you say to the angel is not "I've
discovered the secret of the universe!" because they'll know
that already because they're an angel. What you say to the
angel is: "bridge, bottle, orange, jug, pen." Wim Wenders
understands this in his *Wings of Desire*: what appeals to angels
is the ordinary. So art can be about the condition of ordinary
things, and let those things thing.

TMcC: There's a wonderful moment somewhere in Derrida, which I think you cite in one of your books, where he talks about engagement with the world as being like a dredger that goes through and pulls up the sand beneath the sea, but ultimately lets most of it slip back and "sand."

SC: Yes. There are different ways of being a philosopher or an artist. One is by eating everything and this would be the model of Hegel. It's a caricature of Hegel, and Hegel's obviously better than a caricature. But Adorno has that nice phrase: "Idealism is the rage of the belly turned mind." So the idealist philosopher is like a ravenous belly that eats up the entire universe. The idealist philosopher or artist gorges themselves on reality and shits it out as works that declare the meaning of reality – whether that's the great novel of the modern world or a system of science. The other, contrary model would be to attend to things in their particularity and let them be. Blanchot's point is that we can do neither. So most art is characterized by an ambiguity.

TMcC: My organization, the International Necronautical Society, is massively indebted to Blanchot, obviously. Not only does his work elaborate the irreducible, impossible paradox you've been describing, but it also conceives of death as a space and literature as a space. But I wonder if one could say that the two spaces are equivalent for Blanchot, or are they like two bits of acetate that slide over one another?

SC: What Blanchot is trying to attend to in his work as I see it is a relationship to a space of *dying*, which can't be controlled or appropriated by the human self. And so literature, for him, is the exemplary way in which that space is to be attended to. There might be other ways of attending to it – visually, or whatever – but for Blanchot literature has this overwhelming privilege.

101

TMcC: I love that expression "attend to." Blanchot uses these avatars that attend to it, most notably Orpheus. Blanchot's interpretation of the Orpheus myth is different from the popular one. Blanchot's Orpheus does not go to the underworld in order to get Eurydice back. What he really wants is the night at the heart of the night, the other night, the night whose face is eternally turned away. He wants death itself, in its full absence and deathness. And another trope crops up at this point: sacrifice. That seems an enormously loaded figure, or motif. How do you understand it?

SC: It's not a term I've used. I'm very hesitant about that, mostly because of the question of the holocaust. "Holocaust" is the Greek term for sacrifice, and is, as many Jewish historians have pointed out, a rather questionable way of naming that event of mass death. Sacrifice of what to whom?

TMcC: Sacrifice takes place within a proscribed system of exchange.

SC: Yes, exactly: sacrifice has a meaning that's recuperable. There's a lot of discussion about the uniqueness of the Holocaust, or the *Shoah*, or whatever we call it; but it seems to me that that uniqueness could only consist of one thing: the application of technology to mass death. The curious thing about the Holocaust, in comparison to other forms of mass death – in war, or what was going on in Rwanda or Kosovo – is its dispassionate relationship to death. The Nazis didn't really hate the Jews with a passion; they thought they were vermin that had to be exterminated, which is different. They didn't hate them the way a Kosovo Serb *hates* a Kosovo Albanian; other forms of genocide seem to be premised upon that passion. What's unique about the Holocaust is the attempt to depersonalize and take the passion out of death, and turn it into this industrial process.

Now, we could see that in some sort of weird continuity with the ambitions of the modern world. This is how Zygmunt Bauman sees it in *Modernity and the Holocaust*. Basically, there are two views on the Holocaust: it's either the outcome of modernity or it's a *novum*, something new in history. I think both are true. It's an outcome of modernity: as Adorno says, it's a consequence of rationalization. It's the dialectical underbelly of the rationalization processes that we associate with the Enlightenment. Or it's what someone like Fackenheim sees as a *novum*, a new event in history. Now, that completely reorganizes, and should reorganize, the way we consider philosophical and artistic creation.

If I could go back to what I was saying about Nietzsche: what people get excited about in his work is this notion of affirmation, an affirmation in relation to death. I can affirm the meaninglessness of the universe and the ultimate meaninglessness of my own life, and heroically assume that. There's something almost disgusting about that thought after the Holocaust, it seems to me. Adorno puts his finger on this quite well in the final part of *Negative Dialectics*. He's concerned with "after Auschwitz." He says that a new categorical imperative has imposed itself on humankind: not to let Auschwitz repeat itself, and not to hand Hitler posthumous victories. He goes on to say that the situation of the death camps is best described not by descriptions of them, but by – for example – the work of Beckett. Why? Because it doesn't attempt to represent what took place.

So then there's this question of death and representation: What would be the least disgusting aesthetic response to this situation? At one end of the scale, we've got Spielberg and *Schindler's List*, which for all its sincerity is a disgusting film. At the other end, we've got, say, *Remains of the Day*, which is all about processes that are bound up with what becomes the Holocaust, but it's much more oblique. Or, in the French context, Lanzmann's *Shoah*.

TMcC: That's the eight-hour epic . . .

SC: Right. Lanzmann's aesthetic, which is organized by lots of these concerns I've been talking about, is that he's not going to represent what happened and he's not going to judge what happened. He has interviews with, for example, an SS officer who was at one of the camps, and he's got a hidden camera; and the SS officer wants to either say he's sorry or exculpate himself from guilt – but Lanzmann says, "No, I've got no interest in that; I don't care about what you feel. Just tell me what happened. What happened when the trains arrived? Who opened the doors? How did people get from there to there? How did they get into the rooms? Who put the Zyclon B in? What happened to the bodies? Who dug the ditches? How deep were they? How many?" – these kinds of things. So there's a sense in which that attention to factual description without representing the event would be adequate to that event. So to go back to the question: the way in which we'd be able to approach death is by not representing it, having an oblique relationship to it. So some cherished philosophical ideas of death, heroic ideas, would be gone. Beckett is interesting because he's the anti-heroic figure.

TMcC: In Paul Perry's reading, Beckett puts all the markers in and then takes them away at the last minute. In the first draft of *Happy Days*, for example, the play started with a nuclear blast and a radio voice saying "Nuclear war has been declared; London's gone, New York's gone," etc. – and then Beckett just cut that but left the post-apocalyptic landscape intact. You get that throughout Beckett's oeuvre. There are points where he almost spells it out, like where Vladimir says to Estragon towards the end of *Waiting for Godot*: "Can't you see the bodies piled up in mounds? Can't you smell the decomposition?" He could almost be talking about

Auschwitz. Come to think of it, it's almost like Nietzsche's madman in the marketplace.

SC: Or the farmers in Cumbria!

TMcC: Ah, well, this all opens up to another term I want to bring in, not least because I know you're writing a book about it at the moment.

SC: Yes, it brings us neatly to humor.

TMcC: Beckett is also incredibly funny. It's not a separate thing. His deep ethical engagement with this whole problematic and his humor are completely bound together. How do you see comedy and death as fitting together?

SC: They're in an intimate relationship. Comedy is much more tragic than tragedy, I always think, and much more about death. Tragedy is about making death meaningful – with some exceptions: you could say that in Sophocles' *Oedipus at Colonus* there's a different relationship to death. But conventionally the tragic hero takes death into him or herself, and it becomes meaningful; we experience catharsis in relation to that, and we all go away happily. Comedy is about the inability to achieve that catharsis. So either you can't die in comedy, which is why *Waiting for Godot*'s a tragic-comedy: nobody can hang themselves and it's funny. Or if they do die, they pop back up to life, like in *Tom and Jerry* cartoons. Now, what's the more tragic thought: life coming to an end or life going on forever? The latter's much more tragic. Swift explores this in Book Three of *Gulliver's Travels*: there are the Immortals, the Struldbrugs, who are marked with a red circle in the middle of their foreheads, and lie around in corners having lost all interest in life and not even speaking the language they grew up with. They're tragic figures. The worst thing would be not death, but life carrying on for ever, and comedy's about that. It's also linked to depression and all sorts of things like that.

What's great about Beckett is that you're given the high drama of European culture through a strangely comical Anglo-Irish lens, which is much more pragmatic and down to earth. Beckett's ridiculing to some extent: his laughter is a laughter of derision, a sardonic laughter, which is actually much more tragic. Jokes leave you in that position. The philosophically most nuanced discussion of Beckett is Adorno's, by several kilometers. But what Adorno will not see in Beckett is the laughter. Adorno will say things like "Laughter is the fraud practiced on happiness," "Laughter is complicity with domination." I think that's a mistake. Blanchot also misses the humor in Beckett. The humor in Beckett is at the level of idiom, in the fine grain of detail. There's all sorts of stuff that we might want to call "Irish" – although that would be too easy, but something like that – and it's that that philosophy misses.

TMcC: I see the humor in Beckett as being slapstick, too. That's the element he's getting from Buster Keaton. It's sort of like Bataille's reading of Hegel. Hegel is all about the elimination of matter, turning it into golden shit as you say. But with Bataille, matter becomes "that non-logical difference which is to the economy of the universe what crime is to the economy of the law." It's something that gets in the way of the perfect *Aufhebung*, or synthesis, or resolution. And I think that much of the slapstick in Beckett is about that failure: the failure of tragedy, the failure of matter to get *aufgehobt*, to go up there and be sublime. We want to go to the heavens as heroes, but we trip over our own shoelaces and piss ourselves.

SC: Exactly: we're human.

ANTHONY AUERBACH: The thing that stands out most from Adorno's writing about Kafka is his interpretation of jokes. He doesn't say that Kafka is hilarious, but he still sees jokes as very important. Do you think there's a connection between Beckett and Kafka in that sense?

SC: Well, Kafka is the man. For Blanchot, too, Beckett was nearly, but not quite, Kafka. The measure of anybody has to be to be Kafka. I think you can read Kafka in different ways. As a naive eighteen-year old, I read the novels in English and got filled with existential angst; but then when my German got good enough I read the *Erzählungen* and thought: "How did I ever take this seriously?" I mean, a man wakes up to be turned into a giant beetle!

TMcC: But it seems to me that in Kafka, often, redemption *happens*. It's quite Christian. Josef K realizes "Oh yes, I am guilty," and reconciles himself to his death. It's almost a heroic death.

SC: "Like a dog." What's heroic about that?

TMcC: Well, the deaths in the *Iliad* are pretty gruesome too. Look: Vladimir and Estragon sit around saying: "If Godot comes, we'll be saved." But he doesn't come – whereas for Josef K, there is a kind of martyrdom.

SC: I'd want to get much more Hebraic than Christian at that point. I think it's about inexpugnable guilt. But here's a good story: Georg Lukács was not a fan of Kafka, because Kafka was a modernist and his fiction couldn't be said to coincide with the ambitions of socialist realism. Lukács was in the Hungarian government in '56; he was the Minister of Culture when the Soviets rolled in and came in the middle of the night for him and the other ministers. So he's taken from his bed into a truck, which went out into the country; and he turns to one of his colleagues and says: "*Kafka war doch ein Realist!*" – "Kafka was a realist." So Kafka's fault – that he wasn't a realist – was made up for by the fact that reality confirmed him.

AA: It's like Benjamin's proclamation that the ideas of Kafka will only become known to the masses at the point of their annihilation.

SC: Yes . . . Philosophy is like Flaubert's *Temptations of Saint Anthony*, in which Saint Anthony is prey to various temptations, the last of which is the Spinozist God appearing. Philosophy's like that: there are problems with, say, Kant's philosophy – maybe 30 or 40 which we could identify straight off – but what interests me is the way in which that system can represent a temptation, one that you can take on board. When you're teaching philosophy, you want people to be tempted by forms of thought which are not their own, and then to come to a position from which they can reject them. The idea of philosophy being wrong doesn't interest me, though.

AA: So are you teaching temptation or aestheticism?

SC: Both. You want people to be tempted, and you want them to sublimate. If you're going to do philosophy, you're going to have to spend eight hours a day reading books, which is the most bizarre way to spend one's time; it's a type of renunciation. But at the back of that there's something else. Every great philosophical system constitutes a temptation that is neither true nor false; it's open to a variety of interpretations. A great text is like a machine capable of producing multiple interpretations.

AA: So what of this anxiety about truth? What's the difference between knowledge and truth? Is it all just a game?

SC: No, not a game. Philosophy is about the truth. I don't want to diminish that. Teaching the history of philosophy, though: is that the history of truth or the history of falsehood? It's both. Plato was wrong about all sorts of things, but there's a truth there in that it led to certain things that came after it. So teaching is about using philosophical texts to break down people's convictions about truth in the name of truth. Students usually know what the truth is early on; you have to break that down by saying, "Look, try to imagine inhabiting the world that Descartes inhabited; take that on board as a possibility, even if that conflicts with your intuitions."

TMcC: I wonder if we could rehouse the whole question of truth, and of approaching truth, by taking it out of philosophy and rehousing it in literature. In tragedy, for example: Aeschylus has this formulation, in *Agamemnon* . . .

SC: Suffering into truth.

TMcC: Yes: the gods love us, and so they make us suffer – and the reason they make us suffer is so that we may learn the truth. It's very straightforward. That's the formula of tragedy. It takes place in time, and time is the horizon of decay, whether this is in Faulkner, or Beckett, or Aeschylus.

SC: And in the past.

TMcC: In what sense?

SC: A mythical past.

TMcC: Okay. But it's always this movement towards truth. And then in other types of literature – say in Kafka: the court of the emperor in *The Great Wall of China* is like the angels in Rilke, or the gods in Aeschylus, the place where truth is. There's that same impossible gap: I want to be in the court of the emperor, to be taken up and clasped to its breast, so that I may behold it and join with it; and yet I'm not. It's the same movement, the same thrust. So I wonder: is that *rapprochement* you get in literature parallel to the movement towards truth in philosophy, or is it one and the same?

SC: Yes. Philosophy doesn't begin with people falling into ditches and looking at the stars. The pre-Socratics are interesting; but philosophy *really* begins in drama; it's a competitor discourse to tragedy. Which is why Plato's *Republic* excludes the poets: they're the competition; gotta get rid of them.

TMcC: He says: "We'll deck them in flowers and give them the best wine . . ."

SC: Yes: and then kick the bastards out!

This interview was previously published on the website of the International Necronautical Society (INS).

7 Confessions of a Punk Rocker

Can, Rhythm, and Transient Joy

Julius Nil (aka Seth Cohen)

RESONANCE FM STUDIOS, LONDON, JUNE 2005

In the following interview, Critchley speaks about his passion for music in a manner less directly philosophical than other interviews in the collection. Critchley only occasionally refers to philosophy here, and this has an underlying motivation. Elvis Costello has said, "Writing about music is like dancing about architecture," which is to say, music does not depend upon philosophy. If music is one of the impossible objects par excellence, *this means that it has its own integrity, its own logic, and its own history. Yet, it should concern the philosopher insofar as music is an object that might produce an experience of epiphany and press the limits of reason.*

The interviewer, Seth Cohen, is a New York musician who ended up in London after having played under a series of aliases in Chicago. After encountering Critchley at a lecture on the poetry of Wallace Stevens, he invited him to be a guest on his radio show One Reason to Live *(which Cohen produced under the pseudonym Julius Nil). "As a guest on the show, you would give Julius one reason to live, which was one piece of music. Because I hadn't talked about music much in this format, I picked 'Halleluhwah' by Can because it lasts for 18 minutes. I figured this would take up most of the hour!" Can was an experimental rock band formed in Germany in the late 1960s, influenced by minimalist composers such as Terry Riley and Steve Reich – and two of the original members had studied*

111

under Karlheinz Stockhausen. While Can is not widely known to the public, it has exercised an immense influence on bands and artists such as Joy Division, Talking Heads, and David Bowie. Recently, the music of Can featured in the film Norwegian Wood.

For Critchley, listening to Can, and especially the song "Halleluhwah," produced an almost corporeal effect: "I like this piece so much because there was an epiphany of experiencing rhythm for the first time. In the opening minutes of this incredibly long track, I could feel the drums and bass having some sort of an affective effect on my body and brain in a way I had never experienced before. It was just amazing, and I've never forgotten that." The interview took place in a tiny studio just off the Charing Cross Road.

JULIUS NIL: So what music have you chosen for us today?

SIMON CRITCHLEY: I've chosen a piece called "Halleluhwah" by Can from the album *Tago Mago*.

JN: Why "Halleluhwah?"

SC: It's the piece of music that leaves the strongest impression on me. I heard it when I was 14 or 15 in a friend's bedroom. I can remember the transformative effect it had on me. It was the first time I really understood what rhythm was about. I can remember that distinctly and I've heard it over the years and it's the bit of music that I go back to from those years and it seems constantly fresh to me.

JN: Was that your introduction to Can, hearing "Halleluhwah?"

SC: Yeah, it was a friend of mine called Andrew Faden. I was in his bedroom. His brother was away at university; he was a little bit older and had got hold of progressive Krautrock from a distributor – I think it was United Artists that did this in the UK but you used to get German music through Virgin when Virgin were just starting up. They started as a music importer so they used to carry a lot of Can stuff and I heard it. I suppose I listened to the whole album but I remember the beginning of track 4, "Halleluhwah," and the hypnotic effect of the drums in particular, Jaki Liebezeit's drum style, which is extraordinary, and, yeah, I constantly go back to it.

JN: What else were you listening to at that time? Did this come completely out of nowhere for you?

SC: I was born in 1960, and I ended up going to a grammar school in the north of London and then you had two options: you were either a soul boy, if you were working class, or you were a hippie if you were middle class. And if you were a hippie, you were obliged to listen to Pink Floyd, who lived up the road. My carpentry teacher knew them and we actually met them on a school visit. Or you listened to Genesis or Led Zeppelin and, because I wanted to be a little bit different and exceptional, I got into German music. I think Tangerine Dream was the first thing I got into and then maybe it was Can and the bands like Neu!, Kraftwerk, Amon Düül II and a whole bunch of others, and people like Klaus Schutze, and it was a whole scene. But I suppose Can and Kraftwerk are the two things that are more important to me because they've been threads through subsequent musical history. So you can basically see the influence of this track in sort of post-punk material, Public Image, where they were consciously trying to imitate the drum sound, and you know Jah Wobble ended up collaborating with Holger Czukay, the bass player from Can. And through to Acid House and the whole Manchester scene where you've basically got the rhythm of "Halleluhwah" being aped. I think there might be a Stone Roses' track or Happy Mondays' track, which is exactly the same rhythmic structure. So it's this thing where you've got the germ of dance music and very basic rhythmic organization and combined with that you've got the experimental, avant-garde edge of these students of Stockhausen, like Irmin Schmidt who was the keyboard player, and of this weird guitar style. And the vocals of Damo Suzuki, which are extraordinary because they are either in Japanese or they are completely meaningless. So what that taught me was that it was all about the sound of words and not about lyrical content. So, when I ended up playing in bands a few years later, I got very much into phonetic structures and just making certain sounds. And people like Brian Eno were doing that then. A lot of that came through when Eno split from Roxy Music and started doing things with Robert Fripp early on. It was somehow of a piece back then, all these bits of musical culture. I think you can basically see a lot of things just fan out from Can. And also sampling, of course, that's the other key thing. They were using this two-track studio in very primitive conditions in Cologne and they were sampling. Holger Czukay did all the engineering and all the production. They were sampling – he was sampling – radio and TV signals and other bits of music, very early on, and trying to splice them into bits of music. And they also had this extraordinary thing called the EFS series, the Ethnological Forgery Series – of which there are a couple of hundred numbers, but I think I've heard maybe 30 or 40 tracks – where they imitate North African styles, or Malaysian styles. You've got also the beginnings of World Music, but a conscious imitation of other styles. So it's an extraordinary moment, I think. And also it's against the backdrop of that generation of Germans who were facing up to the historical disaster of Germany after the war. You know it takes 30 years before it really begins to sink in. So you've got the mixture of historical trauma, political radicalism, musical experimentation and drug culture and all that, sort of coming together in the background of this. And for whatever reason, Germany in that period between

. . . well, Can started to record in, I think, 1968 or 1969 and their great period is until about 1974, but that period in Germany is just incredibly fruitful. It continues through into punk, you know, Deutsch-Amerikanische Freundschaft and Einstürzende Neubauten and that, but it's still – it's a great moment.

JN: Let's talk about the influence of Can on people coming shortly after them, specifically in Britain: Eno, Fripp, even Bowie were influenced to some extent I think by this. And, at least on this program, this brings something full circle as we had a little spate of people, back to back, choosing Eno, Fripp, Bowie, which leads me to believe that for a certain age group – maybe between the ages of 35 and 45 presently – there was a moment for people when music's possibilities were expanded by this sort of thing and maybe we can trace most of that, if not all of that, back to Can and maybe Velvet Underground. So I think that's something that seems to have been a watershed moment for a lot of people who have kept up an interest in music since then.

SC: I think that with Bowie I would have said, obviously, the Velvets were a huge influence. But with Bowie, especially on those albums which Eno produced, the drum sounds are so important. The snare sound on *Low* and the drum kit sounds on *Heroes* may betray certain similarities here. But I think with Bowie the more important German influence is Neu!. I don't know if you know the history of Neu!.

JN: No, I don't know much about Neu!.

SC: Well, Kraftwerk initially were a four-piece band and they did two albums in, I think maybe 1970, 1971, I'm not absolutely sure, which were then reissued as a double album when they got famous. And they were a four-piece band

115

and they were doing guitars, drums, all that stuff and lots of organs and early electronic effects. And then they split into two bands; Ralph and Florian go off and become Kraftwerk and the other two become Neu!, who do a lot more acoustic stuff, and with this they develop this incredibly interesting drum technique. And there's a Bowie track on *Lodger* called "Red Sails," which is a direct homage to Neu!, so that's a big influence. But for whatever reason, this constellation of music coming out of Germany in this period works as a sort of counter-current against progressive rock hippiedom in the early 1970s and then fuses; it influences a whole number of people, and then emerges after punk in a particularly strong way. So I guess the people that you are interviewing are consequences of that, a conjunction.

JN: In a lot of your philosophical work, you talk about philosophy being a response to disappointment, political disappointment on one side and religious on the other. Can is an interesting fulcrum in this discussion, particularly this track called "Halleluhwah" but also the fact of something you mentioned earlier, not only dealing with postwar Germany and that political situation, but also, from what I understand, Can's first performance and first recordings came out of some recordings they did of the student protest in Paris in 1968.

SC: I didn't know that.

JN: Yeah, for their first performance they had some site recordings that Holger did in Paris and they used those to construct a track live in a gallery. And I think that was recorded and subsequently released on cassette only. So, especially if you are thinking of the track "Halleluhwah" and the potential religious ramifications of that choice of title, you do have somebody, a band, throwing themselves right into the midst of that disappointment that you discuss in your work and I wondered how you felt about that?

SC: I think there is a sense in which the musical culture that I grew up in, just by sheer chance, was a consequence of the disappointment of the high watermark of whatever we call it, whatever culminates with Woodstock. And I suppose there is a sense in which punk is an experience of disappointment. Punk is a response to the disillusion of the level of economic and social life, particularly here, and the sense in which the 1970s ended up in the vacuum when the shit really hit the fan in 1975 in Britain, when the Labour government went to the IMF to borrow money and things like that. And then there was the oil crisis and then you felt the sense in which the . . . the question is why does punk not really penetrate in the United States to the extent to which it does in Britain? And I think you have to give a Marxist explanation about that. It's about social and economic conditions; that there is a real economic crisis in Britain and social disintegration, racism and antiracist movements as well. And the disappointment that comes out of that sixties culture of promise, which ended up in a sort of haze of Quaaludes and then the grotesqueness and extreme mannerism of glam rock, and the way in which the entire existing music culture is swept away in the early months of the punk movement. I guess in the States, with the exception of bits of the East Coast and the West Coast – where punk did have some impact – there's too much affluence, different economic cycles.

JN: I think it also speaks to the fact that in Britain there seems to be less of a separation between cultural products and consumers. People feel part of what they listen to, watch, and so on. In America there seems to be a detachment; we watch and listen to bands and think of them as other, and distant and separate from us. The phenomenon of gobbing couldn't have happened in the States because American audiences didn't feel that connection with the performers where they would bodily want to connect with them; there was too much of that fourth wall.

SC: The other thing about Can is that they've had a big influence on music in the English-speaking world but they are not from the English-speaking world. I used to fantasize, when I was 16 or 17, about going to visit them in Cologne and walking into the studio and saying "hello" and "thank you for the music," or whatever. But there was this sense in which Germany was a very, very strange culture for me, and that's complicated by the fact that they were doing things with avant-garde-sounding names like Stockhausen which were terribly intimidating. And also the lyrics – Damo Suzuki again – it's very distant in that sense; the references are not domestic. What's interesting is the way in which those nondomestic references then become very much part of a local music culture.

JN: If we're talking about punk in Britain and its direct confrontation with some of the political issues of the moment, Can didn't take on the issue directly. They could be accused of ignoring them or ducking them, but I wonder if you hear it that way?

SC: The question of the relationship between art and politics or music and politics is a very delicate one and I've got very reactionary views on this, in a way, in the sense in which, as Orwell said, all art is propaganda, all propaganda is not art. I think that the question of the political content of music is a difficult one. I find that, when I was a young punk running around here, the bands that I really liked weren't bands such as the Clash. Actually, it was bands like the Vibrators and the Radiators from Space that I really got off on, who were just talking about silly things. It was ridiculous, nihilistic stuff. And

I've learned to like the Clash since, but at the time I found them rather – they didn't speak to me – I found them rather pompous, actually. So there's that stuff, but also the question of how music would carry a political content anyway. I think you could construct a whole elaborate series of debates in aesthetic theory, going back to debates around Adorno in the sixties, where Adorno will say that Beckett is the only coherent response to the Holocaust because he doesn't talk about it directly. So the idea that art should have an indirect content, an indirect relationship to that which is one way of thinking about music like this. There's nothing political, and lyrically Can have got nothing to say. Again, what I like about them in this period with Damo Suzuki is that the words are just phonetics, constructions. Or they're bits of Japanese or they're bits of gibberish and his voice is playing against the music so completely. And then when they try to write songs in English, they get signed by Virgin, I think, in about 1975. And there is an album called *Landed* and a couple after that and then they have a hit, "I want more." There are still good things on there but they are really missing the point a bit. For me, "Halleluhwah" is about sound and rhythm. What I take from this track is just the first experience that I can remember of rhythm making you excited and that sense of just sheer physical joy that you get through it. I guess if I'd grown up somewhere else or if I had been exposed to black music earlier on, then I think it could have been different.

JN: You say that later they went to English lyrics, but these are English lyrics in this song, they are tending towards gibberish I suppose, but there is a choice still. They are a German group with a Japanese singer, deciding to sing, and they sing in some form of English. And of course Can was also borrowing from lots of other cultures, as well. You mentioned the Ethnological Forgery Series. They were self-consciously and overtly acknowledging this debt to that music, and they had various other cultures. The choice to sing in English though – I've always wondered about that, why not just sing in Japanese, why not just sing in German?

SC: I guess that's just marketing. I would have preferred them to sing in German. What I liked about Kraftwerk is that they used to mix German and English, again in such a silly way, but I found that very compelling. I don't know why they did this in English; I guess they wanted a bigger audience.

JN: I have read – I can't remember which member – talking about when they first started up, they just imagined that they would follow the route that rock bands follow, which is building up to the point where you are playing stadiums and selling millions of records. That just seemed like the path you take and it wasn't a matter of succeeding; that's just how it goes. They did expect to reach an audience like that so I think maybe that was part of the choice. Do you know Duncan Fallowell, the London-based writer who has done some stuff with Can? I read something interesting that he said specifically about this record, and I think largely about this track: "These epics are careless of time which means that they are also careless of space – they give one more room physically, intellectually, emotionally: liberation is one of the noblest features of Can's art." So he's hearing something in the music itself, aside from overt political connotation, which he reads as liberation or emancipatory or something along those lines. So he seems to be thinking along the same lines as Orwell or Adorno, saying that this work is political, even in the absence of anything overtly political.

SC: Epic, I don't know if they are epic. They are long, I mean these are long bits of music. But "careless of time, careless of space," that's good. There is something enormously relaxed about this. It's intense. The rhythm is driving all the way through and the music comes out of improvisation; it comes out of some sort of architecture and coherence to the whole piece. But there is a sense of time passing in a careless way. Can recorded a lot of albums from *Soundtracks* and *Monster Movie* with Michael Mooney, then *Tago Mago* and *Ege Bamyasi* and *Future Days* with Damo Suzuki and then there's tons of stuff after that. But it's those three albums that interest me. There's just that conjuncture of limited recording facilities, Damo Suzuki's voice with those arrangements they had. *Future Days*, from 1973, they described as a summer album. They recorded it in the summer and there's actually some ambient birdsong and things like that, but massively relaxed, open music. There is a sense in which they took their time and this track, you know, the beginning is terrific, but the sense in which you are 12 minutes into it before you are really beginning to get the whole effect. It's difficult to imagine people taking those sort of risks now, being allowed to take those risks.

JN: Can's compositional technique has been described as "instant composition," which I think is a bit of a misnomer. Essentially, what they were doing was jamming, recording it all, and then going back and finding the good bits and then Holger Czukay would edit those bits in various ways, sometimes manipulating them quite a bit. But I think that technique probably led to some of that relaxed feeling in the playing, because if you know that you are going to play for two hours, and then just go back and find the good stuff, you don't have to be on all the time; you just have to work your way up to being on at some point. That does allow for a certain kind of openness of playing. It takes some of the pressure off. You don't have to nail that four-minute song in four minutes.

SC: And also the sense in which Can albums are not consistent – there are high points and low points.

JN: And stylistically inconsistent too, jumping from a track like this to a little ditty in between.

SC: Yes, that's right.

JN: I wonder what you think about this: it seems to me that some of the Can mythos, some of the mystique that has stuck with them to this day, is based on this idea of "instant composition," as if they were marginal in some sense, as if they could walk into a room, you know the four or the five of them, and just knock this stuff out as if they were telepathically composing as they went, which of course is not the case. But it seems that is what a lot of people latch onto about them, that it's not an over-crafted, overworked approach to making music.

SC: I think it can give you that impression. I mean, I've got no idea. I remember reading something at sometime about how much time they played together; they played together constantly for several years. I mean they were playing for hours and hours of the day. So, as a unit, they must have got tremendously used to how each other worked and functioned. But I think these pieces are much more crafted, much more formal in a way . . . no, not formal, much more . . . much more crafted. And I'd really like to know how the edits were made, how the music is actually composed. Because I can imagine this being, I don't know, maybe a jam. Maybe it began live, maybe it began over a series of weeks and then it took on this form. But there are movements in this track which are not accidental and people seem to know what to do. Also what's peculiar are the sounds. You can't work out what instrument is doing what; the bass and drums are doing what bass and drums do. I'd like to talk about that, too, because the bass is amazing. But the guitar and keyboards that are in this – you get this sort of spidery guitar effect with Michael Karoli's guitar. I mean, he's not the greatest guitar player. He keeps wanting to play guitar solos and not quite bringing it off and, when he is at his best, he is doing something which is almost indistinguishable from what Irmin Schmidt, the keyboard player, is doing: this very spiky organ playing. So you can't really tell what instrument is doing what and then they'll drop in things like violin on this track. There are reverse tapes; there are all sorts of odds and ends. I see it as the idea that music would be driven by this utterly compelling bass and drum structure and then you are dropping things over the top of that to make a certain picture.

JN: We're developing a sort of theme here – that a lot of what we now read as the Can aesthetic came out of restrictions in various ways: restrictions in terms of technique with Michael Karoli's guitar playing, restrictions in terms of technical apparatus. The recording gear that they had at the time wasn't good enough to get a big full roomy drum sound, so the drums have a very flat kind of sound. The lyrics and Damo Suzuki's approach to vocals may be restricted in some ways by his mastery of English and so on. So it's interesting to think that what we hear as a really mature aesthetic may have been the result of immaturity in specific areas, which I'm more than comfortable with. I think that is the way a lot of good art . . .

SC: Yes. One of Bowie's albums was going to be called *Planned Accidents*. I think it was maybe *Lodger*. I'm not sure.

JN: Something with Eno, no doubt.

SC: Yes, planned accidents, which is almost a William Burroughs approach to music, that there would be this sheer contingency and chance and the issue is how one assembles the various cut-ups. Which I think takes us to the role of Holger Czukay. He's, as it were, orchestrating all of this, it

123

would appear, and the bass sound is so good. I love this kind of tight . . . I don't know how you'd describe it, I guess it's the sort of bass sound that you are getting at the same time in a lot of reggae tracks as well.

JN: Yes, there seems to be a lot of influence coming from there.

SC: Czukay plays with a lot of limited sounds that he is producing, very deep, and the way that interconnects with the drums is so powerful, I think.

JN: I think it's a kind of primarily rhythmic approach. He's not so interested in note choice; he's not making interesting harmonic choices relative to the guitars. What he is doing is working rhythmically.

SC: And you see that with Jah Wobble, who is obviously as his name would suggest – Tottenham boy that he is – that fusion of big reggae bass sound and what Holger Czukay was up to, with a bit of wobble.

JN: There is a lot of that going on, especially in the sixties, a lot of bass players trying to define the role of the electric bass in their music, whether it be in Motown or reggae. And you do sort of get a divide in bass playing around that time: the melodic players, which lead to such travesties as Geddy Lee of Rush, and the rhythmic players, who are really interested in finding that groove. That definitely seems to be the route that Holger Czukay took.

SC: Well, it's all about finding the groove. And again the other track that I would have played, I mean I didn't hesitate for a second in choosing "Halleluhwah" by Can, but "Cold Sweat" by James Brown and the JBs, again for that drum and bass technique. There's a moment when James Brown and the JBs just decide to do everything on one chord and at that moment in 1969 they start to syncopate the bass and drums and Bootsy Collins is doing something in syncopation with the drummer and funk is born at that moment. They find the groove and that leads to the discovery of the one, you know, in George Clinton, and the idea that music is about the one and the return to the one. "Halleluhwah" is about the same thing. It's about the return, finding exactly the one, that's the one, the one reason to live, that one. And I think the rest of music is, well, I think it's irrelevant, or rather I don't understand how people can listen to music and not be after that one, I suppose.

JN: But that is fairly reductive if you are just looking for that one and, if you find it once, then your job is just simply to repeat yourself?.

SC: Yeah, well, I want it over and over again. And then for whatever reason that gives me the most intolerable joy.

JN: And what is a band like Can supposed to do after they've found it and then want to progress past 1974?

SC: Well, the joy of music is its transience. I've got this idea about music and self-identity, that the interesting thing about popular music, or one of the interesting things about popular music, is the way in which you can tell a certain story about your life in terms of certain musical events. I can think of listening to "Suffragette City," my mother bought "Starman" in 1971/2 and the B-side was "Suffragette City," and I remember listening to that and just not understanding that sort of excitement I was feeling. I can think about a series of ones as it were. "Halleluhwah" would be a big one and through to, I don't know, the first time I heard Public

Enemy's *Fear of a Black Planet* or through to all sorts of things: Iggy Pop. And then you can tell a story of your life in terms of those ones. The other characteristic of whatever we call this . . . popular music, is its transience. I mean Can recorded, let's say 15 albums. I think I've got them all, and there's just that moment when they find that right combination and you can almost feel that rightness disappearing almost as it is produced and I think the history of music is like that, moments of transience. I was a big Velvet fan — that moment around those three albums, you could tell a similar story, from *Tago Mago* to *Future Days*, from the first Velvet's album to the third one.

JN: Just about the same period.

SC: Yes, and then *White Light/White Heat*, that's the moment. That's when they find that sound and then it's gone.

This interview was originally published in Seth Kim-Cohen's *One Reason to Live: Conversations About Music with Julius Nil*, Los Angeles: Errant Bodies, 2006.

8 Art and Ethics

Transgression, Visibility, and Collective Resistance

Miguel Angel Hernandez Navarro

BROOKLYN, NEW YORK; MURCIA, SPAIN, DECEMBER 2010

In the following interview, Critchley discusses the ethical status of works of art. Are art objects different from other kinds of objects in our experience, or worse, are they nothing but mere commodities whose purpose is to claim vast sums of money on the open market? Is the art world a fraudulent mask for sheer profit? Or are there forms of "semi-autonomy" – a term used by Liam Gillick to describe an in-between status that criticizes aesthetic practices, while remaining within them.

Critchley had met Navarro in Murcia, after a cultural festival in the south of Spain where he had been debating with Žižek (see interview six in this collection). Elements from this ongoing disagreement can also be found here; more specifically concerns about political paralysis. Navarro had been working with an innovative contemporary art collective that was well-supported – prior to the recent economic downturn. The interview took place over Skype. "I see interviews very much like soccer. You try to stay fit, and then it's a question of sheer luck. Either things go well or they just don't. And this just went well. It flowed."

MIGUEL ANGEL HERNANDEZ NAVARRO: Let me begin with a broad question of the relation between ethics and art. Most artists seem to work on the borders of ethics. Someone like Santiago Sierra is a good example: his work exploits human beings in the same way as the capitalist system does, hence making the point that art can only reproduce the system. My

question is, "can art be unethical?" Is it possible that something can be a good work of art but a bad social act?

SIMON CRITCHLEY: I would see Sierra as an example of a
deeply ethical aesthetic practice. And it's an ethical aesthetic
practice that is working through the repetition of the system
that oppresses individuals, so it's through the repetition of
the very machinery of exploitation that something becomes
different. I would see that work as critical and also as being
orientated around an ethical demand.

The question you raise here is: "Can art be unethical?"
It's a difficult question because if we think of those artists or
writers that we would think of as immoral, what they do is
often in conflict with a certain moral system, a certain moral
code, a bourgeois morality or whatever morality it might be.
But their work is not in conflict with that system in the name
of some value-free, unethical position, but in the name of
some higher ethical position. And I think of that in terms of
writers like Nietzsche and Bataille.

I have been re-reading Bataille recently, Volume 3 of *La
Part maudite*, the one on sovereignty, and it's very interesting.
There you have got someone like Bataille who is completely
immoral on a certain level, but deeply ethical on another.
In his case, it's an ethics of sovereignty. In Bataille, there is
a very clear sense of an ethical demand; the ethical demand
is to conduct one's life in a way that is not reducible to the
principle of utility, what they call in French *le service des biens*,
the service of goods, since if life is simply reduced to the
principle of utility then everything that we do is a means to
an end. So, to that extent, someone that we could think of as
deeply immoral, like Bataille, is profoundly ethical.

I think artists can be cynical. You can believe that what
you are doing has no moral value; you're just having fun or
being ironical or something. This is an unethical position
that I'm personally really tired of. I think that artists can be

immoral, and perhaps they should be immoral; and artists can be cynical, and that's something that I think they shouldn't be, because if art is just about the production of a sort of knowing irony, a knowing distance whereby you rip people off by getting them to spend money on your work but you think that they're stupid, that's terrible. But I don't think that art can be unethical. I think that interesting art is always ethical. It is organized around ethical demands. What that ethical demand might be is up for grabs.

MAHN: You have been talking about ethics and morality. Of course, these concepts are not synonymous: ethics has to do with a position and morality is related to a system or tradition. Are you saying that art can be ethical beyond morality?

SC: Yes, exactly.

MAHN: So it is possible for an artist to go beyond ethics, even when ethics is something that has to do with a subjective demand. I am thinking in some extreme examples of contemporary art, particularly of Zhu Yu and his extreme performances, eating dead babies.

SC: I think that the history of experimentalism in art in the twentieth century is a history of different sorts of ethical engagements, so I think that eating dead babies . . . It could be done cynically. It is certainly immoral, but I'd say it's the articulation of a certain ethical demand that the artist thinks should commit him to the process that his practice is part of. I give this example in *Infinitely Demanding* when I talk about the Marquis de Sade.

The Marquis de Sade was immoral but he wasn't unethical. He thought there had to be a different ethical demand. For him, it was this question of what he called in his late works *Le Droit de Jouir*, the right to come or the right to have an orgasm. So we could dispute that right, but he is as ethical a thinker as Kant or anybody else. I think that it's possible for an artist to not reflect on their practice and just do it, and there are certain examples – like the young British artists from the 1990s – where we find the cultivation of an anti-intellectual, anti-reflective attitude. It's all about making money and the identification between the art world and celebrity culture and pop culture. But I think that's stupid. The artists whom I know and have spoken to, or whom I admire, are all trying to perform their practice in relationship to a demand, a commitment, whatever that may be. So I guess art cannot be unethical.

MAHN: In your work, you give a special role to "action." For you, the only solution in this world is to do things. However, sometimes art is understood as that which is contrary to the production of "actions" or real movements. In our contemporary world, art is often discourse about injustice, about the thing we would like to change, and it only occasionally produces "action." Do you think art can be ethical without action? Do you think action – if we understand it as an instantaneous movement – is a feature of art? Or are there other meanings for "action"?

SC: The political tradition that I come out of, and the political views that I am trying to criticize, leads me to what you were saying at the beginning. A huge early influence on me was Heidegger, and Heidegger's late work ends up in a sort of experience of waiting and inaction. We need to cultivate a disposition of passivity and action, and the will is something we need to be cautious about. For example, in Badiou's work, which I very much admire, there's a sense that we have to wait for an event. An event will arise or it won't arise, but we can't will it into being. For someone like Žižek, the hero is Bartleby, the figure who refuses action. Now I understand why Žižek picks Bartleby as a hero. There is a deep point to that. In Melville's story, there are certain forms of action that need to be criticized, so I agree with Žižek there. We live in a world where there is a relentless imperative to act – to act now – and what we need is reflection and thought, sure. But that shouldn't lead to paralysis. There is a tendency in a lot of contemporary theory to accept a form of paralysis or inaction. We find this in different ways in Badiou, Agamben, and Žižek. But the tradition that I come from is very much influenced by Gramsci. After the First World War, it was clear that the revolution wasn't going to happen in the way the western Marxists thought. In places like Italy, it meant that the whole question of the political – and what political action meant – had to be rethought. Gramsci tried to do that with his concepts of hegemony. But what remains central to someone like Gramsci is that it becomes a question of how we put together a conception of action in concert, across a whole number of disparate interest groups. So for me politics has always been about the expansion of our imagination when it comes to the capacity for action that we possess. And to that extent I remain optimistic in a strange way: I think that human beings acting in concert, acting collectively, have an extraordinary power that they are not aware of. In the face of eventual defeat, there is still this ability to cultivate action and that's very much what I want to do. It's not a question of action for action's sake. So to that extent I agree with Žižek. But I don't think that we can just sit back and do nothing.

MAHN: In your work you link ethics with engagement and commitment, and you speak about the issues of resistance and visibility. In *Infinitely Demanding*, you suggest that politics is a way of "naming," to give a name to a particular situation and to articulate a position of universal hegemony around it. Nevertheless, in other places – especially when you talk about radical groups – you argue for invisibility, where invisibility is resistance in the face of a politics of control. For example invisibility as politics versus visibility as police, using Jacques Rancière's formula. How would you articulate a political position between visibility – having preservation of action through a position and a name – and the preservation of action through invisibility?

SC: It's interesting that you put it like that, because there is a change in my position between *Infinitely Demanding*, which was written between 2003 and 2005, during which time I was reflecting very much on what was happening with the so-called antiglobalization movement, and some other more recent texts. There has been a change in what resistance and protest might mean at the present time. I think that at one level Rancière is absolutely right: there is this opposition between *la police* and *la politique*. *La police* is always about the making invisible of *la politique*. Politics is the emergence into visibility of that constituency which has no part. So politics is that activity of the emergence of a group into visibility. I think that's right – and that can be done through the act of naming: by nominating something, by naming something, I bring it into being. The issue that's on my mind in *Infinitely Demanding* is that we lack a name in politics. What might count as a name? But if we can find a name, then we can, as it were, make that name visible as a group, which means that politics is a poetic activity. Politics is an artistic activity. Politics is about the creation of a name out of nothing, which brings a certain group into being.

Politics is a struggle for visibility. So, if you like, end of story, at one level. But the question that has been raised, the doubt that I have about that now that is expressed in some recent work, is whether visibility is the only strategy of resistance or whether we can think about invisibility as a strategy of resistance. This is not just a change of position. It is also a change that is taking place amongst activists, which I think is also linked to the emergence of new media in the sense in which the antiglobalization movement, particularly after Seattle, was using the technology of the internet, and all the rest, incredibly powerfully. Visibility became a struggle over who controls virtual space, or whatever. Now, I think that those strategies of resistance have become questionable; the limitations of them have become clear. I'm very interested in this idea that you find in the Invisible Committee – in *L'insurrection qui vient* and elsewhere – of politics as a retreat from visibility and the cultivation of an invisibility, an opacity; and also politics as a succession from the realm of the visible. Now I don't agree with that. As I said, I'm a Gramscian at some level, which means that politics has to be about the building up of a front, a hegemonic force; but at this point in history there might be a need for seccession and withdrawal.

Visibility has become completely operationalized or commercialized, it seems to me. Everything is visible. One thing that really interests me as an aesthetic and political practice is those groups or people that are refusing to engage with the internet. There are a number of groups I'm aware of that are circulating texts that are often typewritten or even handwritten, which are photocopied and then handed from one hand to another. And then, after a week or two weeks, 30 people have read that. In a sense, we've been seduced by the question of number: you can put something on the internet and everybody can read it and it means nothing. So the question is, "How does something mean something?" How do we form chains of resistance? It might be by going back to other forms of media. These questions for me are issues that are taking form. Something has changed in the tactics of resistance in the last ten years. I'm trying to think about what concepts might be best used to think that through.

MAHN: I completely agree with this "in-between position" but maybe this is more difficult for art, since it is situated in the realm of the visible. How can art "resist" if it is essentially visible?

SC: I think it's a difficult question. I think one example of invisibility in art would be to look at what someone like Tino Sehgal has done. He has rigorously refused the exhibition in the exhibition, which is sort of fascinating. Nothing about the work is visible. The problem with that is that he seems to accept, completely, the imperatives of the institution. He accepts entirely the institutional framework of the Guggenheim or whatever, or even the opening hours of the gallery and just does his work within that context and then it circulates. That is one strategy. I think there are possibly better strategies. For me, the great thing about the art world is the nakedness of its mediation by capital. In a sense, it's obvious what art is about. It's about selling work and making money. And the artist has become the exemplary worker in conditions of late capitalism. The worker is meant to be an artist. To be a worker, it's not enough to just turn up at work and do your job. You have to be creative; you have to be innovative; you have to be flexible; you have to be constantly available. So if you like, the new model of the worker is a model drawn from the artist. And that means that you can turn up at work wearing your Ramones T-shirt, listening to Radiohead on your iPod; you don't have to shave; you can be completely bohemian; you can say that you hate capitalism or whatever. But you're still a good worker, and in fact you're the best worker. There's a sense in which the artist has become the paradigm for work and I want to think about that a little bit to try to recover some discourses around work. There's a rich history of discourse around work, which we need to go back to.

So the question is – if you go back to the example of Tino

Sehgal, who is someone that cultivates invisibility, but not criticality – can there be an artwork or an art practice that accepts the necessity of the mediation of art by capital and yet still is able to maintain a certain critical stance? I think that's the question. The closest I've got to that is a concept that Liam Gillick is using: semi-autonomy. The old model of criticality in, say, modernism was the criticality of the autonomous artwork: the artwork is critical because it has no relationship to capitalism. The other model would be the complicity of art with capital, which is maybe where we've ended up with art in the nineties. Another model – the one that Liam Gillick is talking about – is semi-autonomy, where art is both completely conscious of its complicity with capital and yet, at the same time, tries to subvert it.

MAHN: To some extent this is the idea you defend at the end of *Infinitely Demanding*, especially when you observe the potentiality of working within the interstices of the state. It seems as if working within the interstices is for you the only way of producing resistance. There is not an outside. We are inside governments, inside capitalism, inside the system. Maybe contemporary art is a good example of this way of working within the interstices of power, creating sites for action in places where institutions dominate. Do you think that these "little resistances" that art produces can be under-stood as effective actions?

SC: As someone who read Derrida for many, many years, I have to say that there is no outside, there is no pure outside. There is also no pure inside. The distinction between outside and inside is always unstable. Institutions are fragile and are totally perforated by an outside they cannot control. To go back to Bataille, he is interested in moments of sovereignty that can be articulated artistically – where the outside can punctuate an inside that is determined by utility and money and the circulation of capital. But that's only going to happen for a transitory moment. This is where the paradox of visibility is. Once something works as a subversive piece of art, then it will simply be reincorporated within the system. The Situationists realized this nearly 50 years ago. At this moment in many ways the recession has been a good thing. People – in the economy, in social life, and in the art world in particular – were living a sort of dream, a fantasy of accumulation and all the rest. I think in many ways that the crisis has forced people to reflect on questions of ethics and ethical responsibility at the base of their practice.

MAHN: We are now speaking about interstices and I think the task of the curator is precisely working with these "in-between" spaces. The curator can be seen as someone who articulates different ethical demands: the artist's demand, the institution's demand and the public's demand; and in some way his or her own ethical demand constructed from an assemblage of different positions and interests. How is ethics possible for the curator in this battlefield of demands?

SC: My first experience of curating was last summer. I did a show at APEX art in New York. It was called *Men With Balls – The Art of the 2010 World Cup*. I was asked by a gallery to do something and I said I just wanted to create a space where we could watch football together. And then we began to put this whole show together. I experienced directly the conflict between those three levels: between the institutional demands, the demands of the artist, and the demands of the public. So I guess curatorship is a sort of compromise structure. I found the experience of being a curator demanding, which is interesting. But in many ways what I was trying to do was to bring about some sort of experience of sociality; that's what I wanted to do. I wanted to create a group of people within a city full of strangers who would watch games together and we would then maybe think about the meaning of this: what is soccer and what is this activity that we're engaged in? What was interesting is that so much of my thinking had to become spatial. I had to think in terms of the organization of space and the management of space, which is not something that I normally do.

On the other hand, those demands I guess are just irreconcilable: institutional demands, artistic demands, and public demands are things which can be momentarily assembled into a show and, then, that's as close as one can get.

MAHN: So you find a sort of infinite conflict or disagreement that has to be articulated. To pose the question again, what is the role of interstices in this conflict?

SC: People often get this wrong in relation to *Infinitely Demanding* and the argument I'm making. My claim is that there are no interstices. The societies that we live in, more or less globally, are increasingly defined by an apparatus of security. That apparatus of security is the control of visibility that is based, say, in the United States, on the fear of terrorist attacks and all the rest. Far from the state being a less important actor politically, it seems that the state is an apparatus that is there to control security at all costs. Within the state, there are no interstices, there can be no interstices. If interstices appear, they have to be controlled, they have to be policed. That's why in the major cities of Europe, we have to know where the immigrants are, the police "have to" be put there; there cannot be interstices. The interstices must be created through an articulation. So, this is something that people often get wrong, and it's not that we can retreat to the interstices, because there are no interstices. The activity, the action, is what creates a momentary interstice; it's what creates a momentary gap. To that extent, a show could do that. An instance of curating could create such an interstice, such a gap.

MAHN: You mean a sort of event?

SC: Yes, the ethics of curating would be the ethics of, as it were, bringing about such interstices within the structure, given the conflicting ethical demands that one is under.

MAHN: But here we have the risk of creating fixed interstices, capable of founding "traditions." And when an interstice becomes something fixed, its critical and political potentiality start to disappear. In your book, you advocate performative acts, modes of resistance that do not aim to create fixed structures. Art is always in danger of canonization. How can art be absolutely contingent? How can we avoid *habitus* (in Pierre Bourdieu's sense of structuring structure)?

SC: There is no answer for that. The risk always exists. We have to be alert in every case. Maybe we have to remember now Jean-François Lyotard. As you know, he curated his very influential show in 1985 called *Les immatériaux*. There was a plan for a second show at the Pompidou, which was never realized because he died, and it was going to be called *Résistance*. I think in many ways the perpetual ethical demand is the creation of Lyotard's posthumous show, to create this show after his death.

This interview also appears in *Manifesta: Journal of Contemporary Curatorship* 12, Spring 2011.

9 Tragedy and Modernity

The Logic of Affect

Todd Kesselman

BROOKLYN, NEW YORK, MARCH 2011

Critchley's relation to tragedy has been ambiguous. In Infinitely Demanding, *he argued that what he called "tragic affirmation" is in fact a misguided response to finitude. Here, however, Critchley returns to tragedy from a different perspective. If philosophy has attempted to define itself, since Plato, through a contrast with tragedy, it is because tragic poetry has an affective dimension that threatens the cold neutrality of philosophical reason. In this context, Critchley discusses the obscure origins of tragedy and the possibility that the tragic employment of affect is now inseparable from philosophical thinking. These thoughts came out of a collaboration with Judith Butler. "I was thinking all this through with her in the context of a course that we have been teaching together at the New School for Social Research, and that experience has been incredibly stimulating. For both of us, tragedy is insight, as well as a source of extraordinary pleasure." The interview, and the forthcoming work, is particularly concerned with the relevance of tragedy for us moderns. Which aspects of this ancient art form continue to ring true for us? Are we, Critchley asks, so very different from the Greeks, and can tragedy serve as a model for contemporary aesthetic practices? This interview is a preview of what is to come. "What's here is whatever the next book is going to be. I just don't know yet."*

TODD KESSELMAN: In Book X of the *Republic*, Plato notoriously excommunicates the tragic poets from his imagined ideal city, thus establishing (or perhaps even perpetuating) the ancient quarrel between poetry and philosophy. What are the stakes of this quarrel, and more importantly, who won?

SIMON CRITCHLEY: Right. A difficult question because, in many ways, tragedy won. The way we normally think about history is that Platonism wins out, the poets are expelled, poetry needs to be defended, Christianity is Platonism for the people, and then there is modernity – something like that. So the usual way of thinking about it is that tragedy loses, philosophy wins. But actually tragedy wins initially. The *Republic* is set sometime around Socrates' death – it's not entirely clear when – but 411 BC is one date that's been given. Ten years later, he is tried and executed by the powers of Athens, and in a sense he's tried by poetry. He dies by poetry in the sense that the discourse which framed the Athenian city, its discourse of legitimation, was theater – tragedy. Other people have said this. Socrates was in a sense killed by poetry, and there is a dramatic critique of poetry in the *Republic*. And so this is just the question of how we understand this quarrel. So at one level, philosophy loses, and moves further and further from the *agora* – which is where, we are told, Socrates engaged in his activity of questioning – to the Academy of Plato, the Lyceum of Aristotle, the Garden of Epicurus and all the rest. Another way of looking at it is that philosophy wins, in the sense in which what happens after the *Republic* is that theater, and tragedy in particular, are looked at from the perspective of a conceptual discourse. And then you've got the enigma of Aristotle's *Poetics*. Is Aristotle's *Poetics* the defense of poetry in prose that Socrates asks for in Book X of the *Republic*? You could see it in those terms very reasonably. Or is the *Poetics* the philosopher looking at the phenomenon of art, and theater in particular, and providing a series of bland, abstract, neutral categories by which art can be assessed? And then you could say, "What Plato's Republic initiates is the discourse of aesthetics," which in a sense begins to triumph.

TK: So would you say that there are two different notions of truth operating here, or are philosophy and tragedy fighting over the same territory?

SC: Right, this is another difficult question. As I see it now – my views on this are changing week by week – there are really two arguments in the *Republic* against poetry. With regard to poetry, I am convinced that the real worry is about theater – and, in particular, tragedy. The two arguments are: first, a metaphysical argument, that tragedy is the imitation of appearances, and therefore is three steps removed from the truth – which is what lies behind appearances in the form of the idea, for Plato. So the first argument is that tragedy is metaphysically untrue because it is imitation. Here we have a clear view of the distinction between a theatrical, or a tragic, version of truth, and a philosophical idea of truth – to reply to your question. The other argument, which I increasingly think of as more important, is that in tragedy there is an excess of lamentation, an excess of grief, and grief as an index for all forms of excessive emotion, of affect. And this is a worry for Socrates because it is appetitive, it is desire, and it appeals to a lower part of the soul than philosophy is meant to appeal to. Philosophy is meant to appeal to the logistical or calculating part of the soul. Tragedy appears to appeal to the desiring, appetitive part of the soul. So the conflict really turns on the nature of affect. Tragedy is potentially politically vicious because it would lead the city to be regulated around excessive affect. And this leads people to live outside themselves – to experience themselves through the suffering of another, the suffering of the tragic hero; they lose control. It is the threat of *ekstasis*. It leads us to lose control of the rational, logistical part of the soul, which is what the guardian and the philosopher should try to maintain at all times. So there seems to be a clear competition between a philosophical idea of truth and a tragic idea of truth. And we can maybe talk more about what that tragic idea of truth might be.

TK: Would it be fair to say that a tragic notion of truth *must* include affect?

SC: Yes. Well, a couple of things. We have a fragment by Gorgias and "The Frogs" by Aristophanes, which stages a debate between Aeschylus and Euripides, but the first philosophical – well, let's say the first systematic – approach to tragedy is Aristotle's *Poetics*. It's weird because Plato says that the problem of art is that it is imitative, it is *mimesis*. And then Aristotle defines tragedy as *mimesis* of an action, which is elevated, composed of several parts, various uses of language; which produces pity and fear, and through the provocation of pity and fear produces *katharsis*. This latter term isn't defined in the *Poetics*; we don't know what it is. Is it the purgation of emotions? Is it like a medical idea? Or is it more of a purification of the emotions, more of a religious idea, or more of a spiritual idea? It's unclear. So for Aristotle, it *is* all about affect. And the first tragedy that we have, *The Persians* by Aeschylus, begins with foreigners wailing with grief. We see Persians in their court, at Susa, crying over the defeat of the Persian army at the Battle of Salamis. News of it has just reached the court and they are wailing, which is typically something foreigners do. Foreigners, for the Greeks, have excessive emotions. It's also an interesting point about affect here, namely that we always ascribe excessive affects to foreigners. So that, when we look at a Shia funeral, we see people wailing and beating their chest. We are reminded of this basic cultural prejudice that we live with. And so many of the tragedies are about lamentation, and grief. And why is there lamentation and grief? Well, usually there's war, and usually – not always, but overwhelmingly – it's the Trojan War. The Trojan War, far from being a source of heroic victory for the Greeks, is seen as a sort of index for something intrinsically problematic in Greek culture. So at the moment of their victory, the Greeks are revealed to be vulgar rapists of a city. The destruction of Troy is always described in terms of rape. A scene that always comes back in Greek tragedies is the abduction of Trojan women, who are taken as slave brides and for sexual favors. The most famous of them turns up at Argos, halfway into the *Agamemnon*: Cassandra.

TK: There's something rotten in the state of Athens?

SC: Tragedy is about the experience of something essentially problematic or rotten in the city-state. Tragedy is very often seen in this way: tragedy is the tragedy of ethical life, what Hegel calls *Sittlichkeit*, the basic tensions that constitute ethical life, the conflicting tensions between man and woman, the private and the public, and so on and so forth. But these tensions are held together in a creative tension, or reconciled in the form of a city-state. And that is a nice story that begins from the idea that tragedy is the art form that expresses the traditional way of life. I don't believe that for a second, though. I think that tragedy is that aesthetic invention that happens when a society experiences itself as being out of joint with itself. There is a certain basic disjunction at the heart of political experience. So to that extent, the Greek tragedies are consistent with the Shakespearean tragedies, which are all about that disjunction between the past and the present, and the sense of time being out of joint, and the sense of there being a basic injustice at the heart of the political order, which is being twisted and worked out in tragedy in some way. That you can't simply say it ends in reconciliation or in destruction, for instance, reconciliation – the *Oresteia* – destruction – the *Antigone*. It's much more

143

complicated and interesting than that. It's as if, for whatever reason, the ancient Greeks were interrogating themselves in this way. For me, the question of tragedy, and it comes up at the end of *Seven Against Thebes*, is: "What shall I do?" The basic question of tragedy is "What shall I do?" Or more generally, if it is the imitation of an action, as Aristotle says, then it is not clear what that action is going to be, and what it means. So, tragedy is that aesthetic form that is able to bear the weight of a world that has become entirely problematic. Again, that is what draws me to it, incredibly, powerfully. Because our situation is not so different, I would argue.

TK: Is there something about the connection between affect and truth in tragedy that is linked specifically to pain and suffering? Does the importance of affect in tragedy rest upon some necessity for putting expression to suffering?

SC: Yeah, I mean, the motto of the *Oresteia*, which makes explicit what's implicit in so many of the tragedies, is that we suffer, suffer into truth. There can be no truth without suffering. And what we see in the various tragedies, are people suffering, or in situations in which suffering has already happened – a child has been killed, a daughter has been sacrificed. And we watch people in the aftermath of a trauma, dealing with that pain. And so, what truth we are meant to suffer into is really unclear. It's not that suffering *is* truth, but there can be no truth without the experience of suffering. That seems to be what we see time and time again. It seems to be that at some level – and this would take us back to this word that I mentioned before that Aristotle introduces in the *Poetics* without explaining it, *katharsis* – there is a process of suffering that seems to lead to an experience of *katharsis*. I want to understand *katharsis* on analogy with the psychoanalytic idea of sublimation. By sublimation, I understand the transformation of affect, and not the loss of affect. So, the common understanding of *katharsis* as purgation would be that we lose the affect, like we lose urine when we go for a leak, or something. It's not that. It's the purification or the transformation of that affect. So the suffering is there, but, through the imitation of action that we spectate, it somehow is transformed. Lacan would say elevated – elevated to the dignity of a thing. Whereas the philosophical discourse on affect, at least in Plato, would appear to be about the threat of affect, which has to be mastered through the rational or logistical part of the soul. That's a very different picture than what we seem to be presented with in terms of tragedy. But we don't know if Plato is serious about this, or if the whole thing is a massive act of irony.

TK: Let me ask a follow-up question here. Aristotle, Gorgias, and Nietzsche all propose a version of the thesis that tragedy is another form of knowing that exceeds philosophical knowing, or philosophical truth. This tragic form of knowing rests upon a connection between *mimesis* and *ekstasis*. That is to say, tragedy is directed towards an ecstatic truth, rather than the truth as clear and rational. What I want to ask is the following: Does this not situate tragedy as an essentially religious phenomenon; and accordingly, could your return to tragedy be seen in terms of a return to ecstatic religious experience?

SC: It is an important question because if we take Aristotle and Nietzsche, all that we know, apart from the archeological evidence, is from the early books of Aristotle's *Poetics*. And he says there that tragedy has its origins in the dithyrambs, in the worship of Dionysus, and it probably does. So theater begins on the south slope of the Acropolis, in the Theater of Dionysus, which was the sanctuary of the god Dionysus. And there was a five-day festival in late March, or early April every year, and this was instituted by the tyrant Peisistratus in 534 BC. We should not forget that theater, which begins with tragedy, is instituted as an official act of the city by a tyrant. There is a connection here between tragedy and tyranny, which is also an argument that Plato makes at the end of Book IX of the *Republic* – so he's not wrong. So on that view, which I think is the most popular view, tragedy is the expression of, or at least has its origin in, Dionysian worship – religious worship. Nietzsche, in what is for me his most perplexing book in many ways, *The Birth of Tragedy* – I see it as a defense of a Schopenhauerian metaphysics that wraps itself in the mantle of philology – argues that the birth of tragedy lies with the Dionysian satyr chorus, and that all the tragic heroes are masks of the god Dionysus. It's unclear, to say the least, whether any of this is true. It's really, really uncertain. And if we say that tragedy had a religious origin, or a beginning in religious ritual, what does that mean? What is it to say that? Is an institution, like theater, which might have a religious origin, a captive to that religious origin for the remainder of its existence? No! All sorts of things have religious origins – the study of law. Universities are institutions with religious origins. That doesn't mean that they are captive to those religious traditions. So for me, the Dionysian side to tragedy has been dramatically overplayed; and along with that comes the idea that the Greeks are Other, the Greeks are these ecstatic other beings that see the world, see themselves, and see reality in a very different way than we do. And maybe they did not experience their bodies, or the relationship of their mental functioning to their bodies, in the same way as we do; maybe they did not have something like a will. I am increasingly skeptical about these claims. Because what is driving them – and this is explicit in the case of Nietzsche – is a violently antimodern prejudice: namely, that modernity is the outcome of aesthetic Socratism, its philistinism, its love of science above all else, with Christianity as its justifying moral discourse. And what the Greeks represent is something completely other than that. So if we can get through Christianity and achieve something like a revaluation of values – we don't become Greeks again, Nietzsche doesn't say that – but we can have the Greeks in our rearview mirror – giving voice to an experience of a pessimistic, affirmative tragic wisdom. Something like that. I just don't buy that. We do not know what the spectator in ancient tragedy saw or thought. We have no evidence and we can only guess. But the more I think about it, the more I think that they were something that is familiar to us and not so different. It's very complicated. They were looking at a world that both wasn't their world, and was their world. Each of the major tragedies – although there are exceptions to this – gives theatrical expression to a disjunction between a time of the gods – Athena, Artemis, and all the rest – and the present of fifth-century Athens. So you've got this bizarre situation in, say, the *Oresteia*, where some goddess or goddesses from way back in the day, maybe from the Mycenaean period – seven or eight centuries before the fifth century when apparently people believed in that stuff – on stage, using the latest techniques of rhetoric and logic to argue with other mythological creatures. And you've got those people who were the chorus, who were meant to be the citizens on stage – and even that is not clear – engaging in some sort of strangely atavistic, choral, religious role. So the gods act like sophists, and the people act like they are part of a religious cult – sometimes, anyway. So the order of time is completely skewed in tragedy and what does that mean? Well, for me it's like what happens when I go to the theater and see a production of *Hamlet*, and a ghost appears on the stage. The question of whether I do or do not believe in the existence of supernatural creatures like ghosts doesn't enter into my head. We are engaged in a theatrical experience, where the order of time is disjointed from the very beginning. So, the same thing for the Elizabethans: when *Hamlet* was produced in 1602 or 1603, what was being represented was some archaic notion of kinship, underwritten by divine order that was in a situation of crisis. Did the spectators of Elizabethan theater point at ghosts and say, "Oh God, that's nonsense. We don't believe in those things anymore"? No, you engage in the deception that is theater. For the Greeks, I think it was very similar. So therefore, the idea of them being exotic, other creatures who believed this weird shit seems to me to be part of an obscurantist antimodern prejudice that we would do well to break down.

TK: So when Socrates is put to death for profaning the gods, it would be something like what goes on in contemporary politics when some Republican claims that homosexuality is an evil sin against God, and then it comes out that they are in fact gay – that there is already a certain kind of political manipulation of belief at work here in fifth-century Athens.

SC: The trial of Socrates *is* a political trial. It's a political trial in a situation, which is – we shouldn't forget this for a second, because this is what makes the whole thing so powerful – a situation of war. The frame of tragedy and the frame of philosophy is war. The first tragedy that we have is from 472 BC: the *Persians*, which I already mentioned, which is about the Battle of Salamis in 480 BC. Most of the plays that we have by Euripides, and a good few by Sophocles, come from the period of the Peloponnesian Wars. The Peloponnesian Wars resulted in the humiliation of Athens by the Spartans, and it was in that context, when Athens was shifting from dictatorship, the rule of the Thirty Tyrants to the restoration of something like democracy, that Socrates was tried and executed. He was inciting the young aristocratic males of the city to acts unworthy of a patriot! So, in a sense, he deserved to die; it was just. The charges against him were legitimate: corrupting the youth of Athens, impiety towards the gods. Though I think killing Socrates was a mistake!

TK: Then, again, you're a philosopher.

SC: Right [laughter].

TK: There's a lot of work one needs to do in order to inter-
pret the Greeks in this way, so here is a two-part question.
First, isn't there something that is tremendously productive
about the fantasy of the ideal Greeks, that in some way actually led to German Romanticism, certain aspects of German
Idealism – one of the most productive philosophical epochs
– based on this very fantasy? Is there something good about
this kind of fantasy? Second, what is the motivation for
closing this gap between us moderns and the Greeks? Is there
something more than just the fact that we can still understand
a tragedy, perhaps in similar terms to that of the Greeks? Is
there something about our contemporary situation that moti-
vates or even necessitates a return to tragedy? Perhaps it has
something to do with technology – the birth of tragedy was
also the birth of a new technology of theater. Perhaps the
connection rests on our own experience of an all-pervasive
technology?.

SC: The first question: the fantasy of the ideal Greeks *has*
been a productive illusion – productive illusion in the
construction of something like nationhood. I forget who
makes this argument, perhaps Silk and Stern in their book
on Nietzsche – it's a long time since I read it: if what the
English and the French had was some sort of idea of a classical age, the sixteenth or seventeenth century for the French,
or the Golden Middle Ages for the English, which could
be a mirror in relationship to which they could then construct a modern nation-state – the Germans didn't have that.
And antiquity then played that role for them. The Greeks
became that mirror in relationship to which the Germans
constructed their German-ness. If you look at poets like

Hölderlin, that whole mirror-play is very evident, and it is true right up through – obviously Nietzsche – but also philosophers like Heidegger. As a way of working out his antimodern rage, Heidegger goes back to an experience of Greek *Dasein*, and Greek uncanniness, precisely as a way of thinking about the relationship of the human being to technology – which he thinks the Greeks had a deeper intuition into. So it is a productive illusion, but it is an *illusion*. Maybe we can't do without such illusions, but it is important to know that they are illusions. The second part of the question is maybe more interesting for me, in the sense of "Why tragedy now?" There are a number of things here. There is a quotation from Bernard Williams's book *Shame and Necessity*, which I really like. It's the last page of that book. He says something like: "We are in an ethical condition that not only lies beyond Christianity, but beyond its Kantian and its Hegelian legacies." And at the end of this quotation he says: "In important ways we are, in our ethical situation, more like human beings in antiquity than any western people have been in the meantime." So Williams's claim, which I want to at least think about, is that we can perhaps learn something from the experience of tragedy because we find ourselves in a similar neighborhood. Namely, that the philosophical idea that there is a pattern or a system that would make sense of human life, with reference to a principle, or a series of principles, or a set of axioms, or presuppositions, or metaphysical essences, or whatever it might be – that philosophical pretension that the universe can be made sense of rationally, has to be given up. History tells us no purposive story, whether it is progressive – the way Hegel tries to imagine it – or regressive – the way Nietzsche or Heidegger try to imagine it. The world was not made for us, or we for the world. We find ourselves in this disjunctive experience that some have called the breakdown of metanarratives. I'm not really sure about that, but you can sort of get that there is some sense to that – a situation of real moral ambiguity, uncertainty, and that fact that things seem to be unknowable with regard to the order of the world. Tragedy can be much more familiar and powerful to us than a philosophical explanation of these phenomena, I would argue. To let the cat out of the bag, for me the core of tragedy, ancient and modern, is the experience of moral ambiguity, where we see in a theatrical presentation that truth is not one thing, but at least two things – and those two things are in a conflict – and not just a conflict, a life-and-death struggle. And we watch competing claims about the ultimate moral ends of human life batter each other to death in this theatrical conflict. And I think that we can learn something from that. We watch whatever justice might mean; we watch it twist from one thing to another thing, in a tragedy. Without being told what to think. We don't know what to think – there is no narrator coming in and telling us, "This is what this means." There is no, as it were, philosophical overview. And this is what Jean-Pierre Vernant calls "tragic consciousness." Tragic consciousness arises with a couple of things. It arises with the acceptance of the idea that we live in a world of our own creating, that theater is the fictionalization of that world, and we can learn from that. And what we learn from it is our situation of rigorous moral and political ambiguity, which leaves us unknowing.

TK: To go back to Vernant's reading, he makes the argument that this moral ambiguity was expressed very specifically for the Greeks in terms of the belief in a regular order of nature – the sun rises, it sets, rinse and repeat – yet at the same time, there is a kind of anxiety in the face of what is totally unpredictable, namely what the gods might dump upon us in terms of fate. And tragedy is what happens when these two impulses, regularity and unpredictability, come into conflict, as you were saying earlier. To push the question

151

of the connection between contemporary life and antiquity, what would be the equivalent forces, or are those forces no longer even clear to us?

SC: Right, I mean, it's a really good question. One of the problems with what I've said so far is, what are the Greeks up to when they are talking about their gods? We don't believe in these gods; we may believe in a god, or whatever, but this sort of perverse polytheism that we find in the Greek pantheon seems strange to us, to say the least. But to go to the question more directly, and to maybe give an example, Vernant's claim makes perfect sense of, say, Oedipus the tyrant – *Oedipus Tyrannus* – which is a meditation on the nature and necessity of tyranny. And the vast question, which we are left with in *Oedipus the King*, is whether tyranny is part of the nature of the city, or whether it is a pollution which can be excised. It's not clear. But we have an idea of there being an order of nature, of things being okay, and of fate having created a whole world of shit for Thebes – bodies are piling up, women are giving birth to stillborn children, the water is polluted, people are dying, there are corpses everywhere – something's up! It's precisely that situation that Vernant describes, the disjunction between the order of nature and fate befalling somewhere. We could make sense of that in terms of catastrophe, the experience of catastrophe. We can make sense of that in the sense of, "if we can't believe in gods, then we can believe in forces, which are outside of our control, which shape our actions, unknowingly." This is what's going on in *Oedipus Tyrannus*. Oedipus' existence is shaped by a prophecy. By the time he gets to Thebes, he knows what the prophecy is and he is trying to escape it; but unwittingly, he fulfills it. A prophecy that unknowingly shapes our existence and shapes the actions that we take in that existence, namely, the action of killing someone at a crossroads, who happens to be your father, and marrying someone, who is the queen, who happens to be your mother. So, what's revealed in tragedy through these prophecies, gods, and all the rest, is a situation where we act, and yet we are acted upon at the same time. Action, and being acted upon at the same time, unknowingly. And that is something that makes perfect sense to me at an everyday intuitive level. We act, and are acted upon, in a specific situation of rage. What happens in tragedy after tragedy – we could talk about *Hecuba*, and other examples – but to stay with Oedipus: Oedipus, in his rage, kills the man who is unknowingly his father because he refuses to make way on the road, and the man who was his father refuses to make way as well. In rage, we act, but we act in a way that we are acted upon, and the prophecy speaks through us. That I think makes perfect sense of what it means to be an asshole. What is the philosophical essence of assholism? It is to act in a way that you are acted upon unknowingly, and in doing that you are repeating, you are playing out some kind of transgenerational curse, bound up with your ancestors, with your place, with your context and all the rest. Or again, these forces could be expressed in terms of Ibsen – in *Ghosts*, that transgenerational curse is transformed into a sexually transmitted disease, syphilis. It can take different shapes. But the idea of action as something we are not fully conscious of, where we do not fully know what we do, would be the key idea in tragedy. And this is where things get even more complicated: we watch someone engage in a process of enquiry, Oedipus, where he learns the truth about who he is – and is that going to make things better? We could think about that, but it's a complicated question.

TK: Let me ask the question about ancient versus modern tragedy. What I was thinking was that one of the things that it seems very easy to identify with now is a kind of Hamletized subjectivity – where we know, but we cannot act. This seems to really describe what has been going on with regard to the financial corruption in the American political context, or we could point to the issue of global warming. Our time seems to be characterized by the strange disjunction between the fact that "we know very well," yet we are unable to effectively act to change things. It is as if we have our own strange version of fate. You're saying that ancient tragedy has something to do with a kind of interiorization of knowledge, or a shift in one's relation to knowledge: Oedipus is told what is going to happen; yet it is somehow still alien to him.

SC: It's strange, because when we think about the play in our heads, we imagine that he is ignorant, and then he knows. But it's much more complicated than that. He is in Corinth, because he thinks that where he's from, and there is a party, someone is drunk and they call him a bastard. This triggers something in his head and he goes off to the oracle at Delphi to find the truth, and he learns the prophecy, and then on the way back he kills his father, and winds up as the king of Thebes. And then when the play begins, Tiresias is brought out and tells him to his face that he is the murderer that the city seeks, that he is the pollution. He doesn't hear it. So part of what is going on in tragedy is that people are being told the truth, and not hearing it. What is going on there? Going back to the phenomenon of assholism, what are the conditions when something is heard? It seems to me in tragedy, part of what we learn is the fact that we don't hear. So with Oedipus, it takes a long time. And when he does hear, when he does know, he still kicks and screams. In the last lines of *Oedipus the King*, he is trying to take his children with him, Antigone and Ismene. And Creon's last lines are, "Do not think that you are a master. You are not a master. Your days of mastery are over." So Oedipus is a tyrant to the end. And then we could give – we don't have to do this now – a whole reading of *Oedipus at Colonus*, where he goes back to being the asshole, all over again, playing out his rage against his sons and his incestuous desire in relationship to his daughters, which then raises the really deep question: "What do we learn from ancient tragedy?" We know what we are meant to learn: we are meant to learn the truth, the truth will set us free, and this comes through suffering. Are we shown situations where people really do learn from the past, or do they not rather keep falling back into that situation of being an asshole? But I want to get back to *Hamlet*. *Hamlet* is something else. Your question is very good because, if there is a difference between ancient and modern tragedy – I am not saying that there isn't, and we've also got to think about Roman tragedy, Seneca, and different things, but let's put that to one side – then it is a difference that turns on the relationship of knowledge to action. A very simple way of carving things up is that Oedipus acts, but doesn't know. Hamlet knows but cannot act. You might want to say that *our* situation of "Hamletization," as Carl Schmitt would say, is a situation of indecision, where we know what needs to be done, and yet we can't do it; except inadvertently. I mean, Hamlet could only act when he doesn't think about it. He sees a curtain or arras move in his mother's chamber, and he immediately sticks the sword through it, and then asks, "Is it him?" thinking it was Claudius. But it is Polonius. And then at the end of the play when he finally does kill the king, it is inadvertent, accidental. So, to that extent, we are Hamletized, we are indecisive, obsessional, impotent creatures that can only desire when it is impossible to do so: Hamlet can only express his desire for Ophelia once she is dead. And he only expresses it in an act of competition with her brother Laertes because he seems to be expressing more grief. So, to that extent we could say, the situation of ancient tragedy represents a different sort of ideal, an ideal of the non-Hamletized existence.

TK: So you can either be a modern neurotic, or an ancient asshole?

SC: Right! But the situation for someone like Orestes, who does kill his mother, is unlike Hamlet. They both know the truth: Orestes can act; Hamlet can't. But again, we're not quite sure why he can't act. It's not clear; why can't Hamlet do it? Why is it that the closest he can get is another act of theater, within the theater, which is the mousetrap play that is supposed to catch the conscience of the king? Why is that the closest he can get?

TK: One account of tragedy is that it is an attempt to teach us something about the way that the world is, and it is either successful in this, or it fails. Another response would be that it doesn't fail because it is not attempting to teach us anything in particular. You've pointed out that there is a connection between tragedy and conflict, decadence, or corruption – not just a topic, within tragedy, but also as a condition for tragedies to be written, and for them to be effective. Given this connection, are tragedies meant to be descriptive or critical?

SC: We want to think that they are critical. We want to think that the deaths in tragedy have significance. There is a great quotation from Anne Carson: "Aeschylus looks at the story of Agamemnon and sees a parable of human grandiosity and tragic catharsis that leads through bloodshed, pain, and suffering to the eventual restoration of the civilized order – the city. Euripides looks at the same story and sees smeared makeup." The smeared makeup option is a powerful option. The play that that remark prefaces, Euripides' *Hecuba*, seems to be pointless! It begins with the appearance of the ghost of her son, Polydorus, who has been slaughtered. Then Hecuba learns that all of her kids, apart from Polyxena, have been killed. But Polyxena is scheduled to be slaughtered as a sacrifice to the ghost of Achilles, who has appeared, demanding blood. And there is very little that is redemptive in the slaughter of Polyxena. Then Hecuba finds out about the death of Polydorus, and, finally, she comes alive through revenge. She figures out a way that she can get back at Polymestor, with her Trojan women. And often what you are presented with in ancient tragedies are groups of captured foreign women encamped with the Greeks. They lure Polymestor into a tent, his children are killed in front of him, and his eyes are gouged out. The revenge focuses her mind. At the end of the play, the blinded Polymestor tells Hecuba what fate has in store for her, which is to be turned into a dog in the afterlife. Now what moral do we take from this story? It's like the end of the Coen Brothers' *Burn After Reading*. You get this extraordinarily elaborate, intricate plot and web of deceit, and at the end, when they are in the FBI office, someone says, "Now, what did we learn from this? Absolutely nothing!" So there is a sense in which there are tragedies where what seems to be playing itself out is a sheer unpleasantness. And pointlessness. And you moralize that at your own peril. The moral in that is that there is no necessary morality to art, for me. The question of whether art is moral or immoral is a philosopher's question, which is of absolutely no interest to art. Maybe some of it is, maybe some of it isn't, but it's not meant to be good for you, like Guinness. It is what it is. Does reading Bataille's *Story of the Eye* make you a better person? It's interesting to read, but it's a more complicated question than that.

TK: Here in Brooklyn, the answer is yes . . .

SC: If only Brooklyn were a concrete universal in Hegel's sense. Tragedy is descriptive, which might also be a way of being critical, so the two things are not mutually exclusive. An awful lot of seemingly pointless death goes on in Greek tragedy. If we begin to take a body count in Senecan tragedy, and Elizabethan tragedy, it is enormous. Why? Why all these bodies? The really difficult question to accept – well, maybe

it's not that difficult, maybe just difficult for academic hypo-
crites like us – is that maybe we just find pleasure in seeing
that suffering. Maybe what is going on in tragedy is that
tragedy is a form of pornography. We get off on virgins being
slaughtered and brides being hanged.

TK: But isn't that another way of restating Nietzsche's thesis
that life is only justifiable from an aesthetic standpoint?

SC: I'm not even sure it is justifiable, in this sense. Nietzsche's
thesis – and this is what is dishonest about the *Birth of Tragedy*,
which makes it a strange book – is this idea that it "is only
as an aesthetic phenomenon that existence in the world is
justified," is itself a Schopenhauerian thesis. There is this
thing called "The Will," which is driving everything, which
aesthetically can throw up a screen that makes it bearable for
Nietzsche. But what that's got to do with tragedy is neither
here nor there. The examples given in *The Birth of Tragedy*, I
find slight. I think it is more that the spectators in the theater
witness a scene of ambiguity that might lead them to learn
something; it might lead them to be disgusted with existence.
So justification is going too far, I think.

TK: What is the essence of tragedy?

SC: Ah, yes. The essence of tragedy. Something, I think, that
we have not mentioned that is important: on my reading,
philosophy begins in Plato's *Republic* with the exclusion of
the tragic poets. It begins as a counter-discourse to tragedy.
When philosophy then enters its period of self-acknowledged
crisis after Kant, the model it resuscitates – as a way of trying
to bridge the gaps between, say, pure and practical reason,
in Kant – is a model of the tragic. In Schelling, in Hegel, in
Nietzsche, in Heidegger, in Scheler. Benjamin pushes back
against this in his wonderful book on *Trauerspiel*. So the

history of philosophy, on a certain perspective, has asked no other question than the essence of the tragic, and there are different answers. This is where I want to go back to two figures, to Aristotle and to Hölderlin, and to link them. The view you find in the work of Peter Szondi in *The Essay on the Tragic* – which is a very interesting book – is that Aristotle gives us a poetics of tragedy, whereas what we find after Kant is a philosophical discourse on the tragic, which is of a higher level. I think that is a mistake. For me, what interests me about Hölderlin, as a figure, is that he is concerned with the praxis of theater. And in his failed attempt to write *The Death of Empedocles*, his translations of *Oedipus the King* and *Antigone*, he is preoccupied with the praxis of theater. And in Aristotle, we begin with this idea that tragedy is *mimesis praxeos* – mimesis of an action. I guess what I am trying to imagine is a praxeological critique of the privileging of the essence of the tragic in a certain philosophical discourse. What most interests me – while the texts are fantastically interesting – is the performative aspect of tragedy. This could perhaps give us an index for a different *praxis* of thought, which wouldn't be fixated on one model of truth, one model of truth that has to defeat all of the others, but where we are presented with a scene, a stage, where more than one model of truth is shown to be in conflict, and we are forced to deal with that.

TK: Szondi says, more or less, that tragedy dies, in the same way that history ends for Hegel. If this is wrong, can we say that a praxeological conception of tragedy is able to account for why, in that moment, looking back at the history of tragedy, it looked as if it had died – but in fact it is more relevant than ever?

SC: Yes. And the death of tragedy thesis is one that I am averse to. You find it in George Steiner and elsewhere. I don't buy it. Again, for me it is part of a sort of – if not antimodern – let's say a reactionary discourse that wants to declare that the best is over, something is a thing of the past and we look back in awe at the god-like creatures that precede us. I mentioned this to you before, but it's important to me. I spent the last month or so watching all five seasons of *The Wire* – which is a great piece of television. I am not saying *The Wire* is Greek tragedy; there are huge formal differences between them. *The Wire* is 50 or 60 hours long altogether. But the experience of necessity that governs the action, the sense of characters acting, yet being acted upon, the feeling of moral ambiguity that frames the action – who is right? Is there a discourse of the law here? Or is there a discourse where the law is in question?

TK: The thing that strikes me about *The Wire* is that it seems to be constantly playing with the thought that things, in actuality, or in reality, could be otherwise, but we know that they won't be. So the very notion of tragic fate is somehow transformed into a kind of immanent fate. It's just as strong as a metaphysical notion of fate, and in some ways more frustrating.

SC: I don't think that it is that different. It's unclear to me at the end of *Oedipus Tyrannus* that the city can do without tyranny. The subject of *The Wire* is Baltimore – the city of Baltimore. Different seasons focus on different institutions that constitute the city: the education system, the police department, the city hall, the political system, and the press. So it adds up to a sort of picture of the city, and I think that ancient tragedy also gives a picture of the city. Can the city do without tyranny, or is tyranny something that the city is going to have to periodically suffer, and the pollution that comes with it, and the city will have to scapegoat in some way? I don't know. For me this is the question – and we are speaking in March 2011 – whatever is going on in North

Africa, which people far too casually describe with the term "revolution" – as if we know what revolution is, and as if revolution is in itself a good thing, neither of which are clear to me. But the shifts, the dislocations, that are happening in those regimes, each of which in a different way are forms of tyranny; we have a situation where a form of sovereignty is being questioned – the identification of the sovereign with the person of the tyrant. That is being broken down. But what will that beget? Will that just beget another cycle of tyranny and some other fresh form of subjugation? It's unclear, and one hopes not. I see the same discourse of hope in ancient tragedy. There's this extraordinary line in *Prometheus Bound* where Prometheus – who gave human beings technology, because he gave them fire and beforehand they were these grey, sort of maggoty creatures, crawling under the surface of the earth, and he made them everything that is worthy – the chorus interrogates Prometheus and says, "Well, what else did you give them?" And Prometheus says, "I allowed them to stop thinking about doom." And the chorus says, "How?" And he says, "By sowing in them blind hope." And there is something powerful about that. That, sure – we hope. But in a tragic sensibility and tragic consciousness, that hope has to be measured against a rich and non-delusive awareness of the past, in particular, and the way the past affects the present. I think that's the lesson. All these disjunctions we see in tragedy, temporal disjunctions, are fundamentally about the way in which the transgenerational curse of the past makes its effects felt, unknowingly, on the present. Could we be free of that? We can imagine that, sure. And maybe it can be sustained. But maybe that is blind hope too. Maybe we are children of Prometheus.

TK: Because I know that it is something that you have been thinking about, is there a relationship between the regular repetition of tyranny and monstrosity?

SC: Oh, right. Well, it's a complicated question. So I am teaching this course with Judith Butler, and her focus in her first lecture was on the figure of Antigone as a monster, and of Oedipus as a monster. And she means this in a very technical sense – they neither have a political identity, because they were kings or daughters of kings, and they've lost that – nor do they have a private identity because there has been a confusion of generations in them, through incest. So both privately and publicly they are nothing. So in a sense what we are shown in tragedy is someone who goes from a situation – in the case of *Oedipus the King*, where he thinks he knows who he is – a situation of delusive knowledge, to a situation of knowing ruination, which leaves him as a monster. What moral does someone derive from that? It's completely unclear. Is there a flaw in Oedipus that we are meant to avoid in our actual lives? That's really unclear. But there seems to be something about monstrosity at work in tragedy. The other figure of monstrosity is in Hölderlin, where he talks about the monstrous as the coupling of the human and the divine. The monstrosity of tragedy consists in this almost sexual coupling that he identifies in the figure of Empedocles. And this is where we begin *Oedipus the King*. *Oedipus the King* begins with someone who really thinks of himself as a god, and he thinks of himself as god because he is seen as great. His first lines when he comes out on the stage are: "You know me, you know who I am. I'm Oedipus, whom people call great, because I solved the riddle." So we go from that delusive knowledge, where knowledge comes from the fact that he is seen, if you like, the knowledge of celebrity and that sort of monstrosity – celebrity monstrosity – to a knowing ruination at the end of the play, where he can't bear to be seen. He puts out his eyes, and he can't bear to be seen blind because of the experience of shame. There is this wonderful Greek saying, which Anne Carson digs up, "Shame lies on the eyelids." And there is something about that in tragedy – tragedy is about watching people move into a situation of shame. So, monstrosity is present at the beginning and the end of tragedy in a very interesting way. Another thought that I am trying to develop at the moment – and I'm not sure what I am going to do with this – what would be the affect that would accompany monstrosity? If the affects of tragedy are meant to be pity and fear, yet there is monstrosity in tragedy, what might *then* be the affect of tragedy? There is this line in Nietzsche, paragraph 7 of *The Birth of Tragedy*, where he talks about disgust as the affect that accompanies the monstrous. And that is something I have been thinking about. What might be an aesthetics of disgust in relationship to these phenomena – which would also take us back to Hamlet? Because what Hamlet feels is disgust. There is this extraordinary moment where he is saying to Rosencrantz and Guildenstern: "Denmark's a prison." And Rosencrantz replies, "Then is the world one." And Hamlet responds, "A goodly one, in which there are many confines." Then he adds, "There is nothing either good or bad, but thinking makes it so." So in a sense, in the modern tragedy of Hamlet, we are shown someone who is monstrous, in his way, and who experiences disgust for everything. And so I still don't know what I'm going to do with that thought, that linking of the tragic, not to the sublime, as is usually the case, but the linking of tragedy to the experience of disgust. So the linkage of the monstrous and disgust is something I am still thinking about. There might be something in it, but that's the best I can do for now.

List of Works

The Ethics of Deconstruction: Derrida and Levinas (Oxford: Blackwell, 1992); rev. and expanded edn, with three new appendices (Edinburgh: Edinburgh University Press, 1999).

Very Little . . . Almost Nothing: Death, Philosophy, Literature (London and New York: Routledge, 1997; rev. and expanded 2nd edn, 2004).

Ethics—Politics—Subjectivity. Essays on Derrida, Levinas and Contemporary French Thought (London: Verso, 1999; reissued in Verso's Radical Thinkers series, 2009).

Continental Philosophy. A Very Short Introduction (Oxford: Oxford University Press, 2001).

On Humour (London and New York: Routledge, 2002).

Things Merely Are - Philosophy in the Poetry of Wallace Stevens (London and New York: Routledge, 2005).

Infinitely Demanding. Ethics of Commitment, Politics of Resistance (London and New York: Verso, 2007).

The Book of Dead Philosophers (London: Granta, 2008; New York: Vintage Books, 2009).

On Heidegger's Being and Time, with Reiner Schürmann, ed. Stephen Levine (London and New York: Routledge, 2008).

Der Katechismus des Bürgers (Berlin: Diaphanes Verlag, 2008).

How to Stop Living and Start Worrying – Conversations with Carl Cederström (Cambridge: Polity Press, 2010).

Offizielle Mitteilungen – International Necronautical Society, with Tom McCarthy (Berlin: Diaphanes Verlag, 2011)

164

List of Works

The Faith of the Faithless – Experiments in Political Theology
(London and New York: Verso, 2012).

Index

Index